SPANISH IRONWORK
HISPANIC SOCIETY PUBLICATIONS
NO. 89

EASTON PUBLIC LIBRARY
EASTON PA

GILDED IRON PULPIT IN AVILA CATHEDRAL.
Renaissance. Circa 1520.

SPANISH IRONWORK

BY
ARTHUR BYNE
AND
MILDRED STAPLEY

WITH ONE HUNDRED AND FIFTY EIGHT
ILLUSTRATIONS

THE HISPANIC SOCIETY
OF AMERICA
1915

COPYRIGHT, 1915, BY
THE HISPANIC SOCIETY
OF AMERICA

TABLE OF CONTENTS

	PAGE
LIST OF ILLUSTRATIONS	vii
INTRODUCTION	xxi
I SPANISH IRONWORK PREVIOUS TO THE GOTHIC PERIOD	1
II GOTHIC REJAS AND PULPITS	20
III GOTHIC HARDWARE AND DOMESTIC-UTENSILS	45
IV THE DEVELOPMENT OF THE RENAISSANCE REJA	69
V RENAISSANCE CHURCH REJAS	80
VI SMALLER RENAISSANCE PRODUCTIONS	102
VII THE LAST OF SPANISH IRONWORK	120
INDEX	131
CATALOGUE OF IRONWORK IN THE COLLECTION OF THE HISPANIC SOCIETY OF AMERICA	139

LIST OF ILLUSTRATIONS

GILDED IRON PULPIT IN AVILA CATHEDRAL.
Renaissance. Circa 1520.   *Frontispiece*

	PAGE
CELTIBERIAN SWORD. Found at Amarejo	1
Fig. 1. EARLY CATALAN FORGE	3
Fig. 2. SANTA CRUZ REJA, Pamplona Cathedral. Early XIII Century	2
Fig. 3. REJA ARABE, CAPILLA DEL SAGRARIO, Palencia Cathedral. XIII Century	4
Fig. 4. WINDOW REJA, Nuestra Señora del Mercado, Leon. Late XIII Century	4
Fig. 5. IRON NAILS WITH WROUGHT HEADS. Moorish. XIV Century	15
Fig. 6. IRON NAILS WITH WROUGHT HEADS. Spanish. XVI Century	15
Fig. 7. DETACHED NAILHEADS OR BOSSES. XVI Century	6
Fig. 8. BOSSES AND KNOCKERS. Count of Toledo's house. XVI Century	10
Fig. 9. IRON-MOUNTED DOOR. Avila. Early XVI Century	10

LIST OF ILLUSTRATIONS

		PAGE
Fig. 10.	COPPER-PLATED DOORS. Puerta del Perdón, Mosque of Córdova. 1377	12
Fig. 11.	DETAILS OF PANELING AND KNOCKER, Puerta del Perdón	12
Fig. 12.	BRONZE-MOUNTED DOORS. From Sevilla Cathedral, now in the Museo Nacional, Madrid. Late XIV Century	12
Fig. 13.	IRON-PLATED DOORS. Main Portal of Tarragona Cathedral. 1510	14
Fig. 14.	CLOISTER REJAS, Barcelona Cathedral. Early XIV Century	16
Fig. 15.	REJA OF A CLOISTER CHAPEL, Barcelona Cathedral	18
Fig. 16.	REJA OF A CLOISTER CHAPEL, Barcelona Cathedral	20
Fig. 17.	DETAIL OF REJA LOCK. Cloister Chapel, Barcelona Cathedral	23
Fig. 18.	REJA, CAPILLA DE NUESTRA SEÑORA DE LAS ANGUSTIAS. Church of San Pablo, Palencia. Early XV Century	24
Fig. 19.	WINDOW REJA. Archiepiscopal Palace, Salamanca. XVI Century	20
Fig. 20.	WINDOW REJA. Casa de las Conchas, Salamanca. 1514	20
Fig. 21.	LATTICE REJA, Puerta del Obispo Tenorio, Cloisters of Toledo Cathedral. Circa 1400	22

LIST OF ILLUSTRATIONS ix
PAGE

Fig. 22. LATTICE WINDOW REJA. House of Pedro Davila, Avila. XVI Century 22

Fig. 23. DETAIL OF INTERSECTIONS. LATTICE WINDOW REJA. House of Pedro Davila, Avila. XVI Century 28

Fig. 24. SPLIT BAR REJA. Patio of the Count of Toledo's House, Toledo 30

Fig. 25. SPLIT BAR MOTIF. Reja of the Royal Chapel, Granada. 1518–23 24

Fig. 26. TYPICAL PATTERNING INTO WHICH BARS WERE OPENED 31

Fig. 27. GOTICO–FLORIDO REJA. Casa de las Conchas, Salamanca. 1514 26

Fig. 28. GOTICO–FLORIDO REJA. Casa de las Conchas, Salamanca. 1514 26

Fig. 29. TOMB REJA OR VERJA. Tomb of Bishop Diego de Anaya, Old Cathedral of Salamanca. Circa 1450 28

Fig. 30. REJA, CAPILLA DE SANTA ANA. Burgos Cathedral. 1488 28

Fig. 31. CLOISTER REJA. Cresting in color, Sigüenza Cathedral. 1508 30

Fig. 32. CLOISTER REJA. Cresting in color, Sigüenza Cathedral. 1508 30

Fig. 33. RUBBING OF UNDER PLATE OF TRACERY BAND 32

Fig. 34. RUBBING OF UPPER PLATE OF TRACERY BAND 32

LIST OF ILLUSTRATIONS

PAGE

Fig. 35. THE TWO PLATES RIVETED TOGETHER. Middle XV Century   32

Fig. 36. RUBBING OF UNDER PLATE OF TRACERY BAND   34

Fig. 37. RUBBING OF UPPER PLATE OF TRACERY BAND   34

Fig. 38. THE TWO PLATES RIVETED TOGETHER. Middle XV Century   34

Fig. 39. FOLIATED BAND. Pierced and Beaten in Repoussé. Late XV Century   41

Fig. 40. FLAMBOYANT GOTHIC PULPIT. Avila Cathedral. Circa 1520   36

Fig. 41. WROUGHT IRON HINGES, Church of San Millán, Segovia   36

Fig. 42. CRUDE DOOR KNOCKER. Probably early XV Century   38

Fig. 43. DOOR KNOCKER. Showing early use of crown motif. Later XIV Century . .   40

Fig. 44. GOTHIC-RENAISSANCE DOOR KNOCKER. Early XVI Century   42

Fig. 45. GOTHIC-RENAISSANCE DOOR KNOCKER. Early XVI Century   44

Fig. 46. GOTHIC-RENAISSANCE DOOR KNOCKER. About 1660   44

Fig. 47. ARCHAIC HAMMER OF A XV CENTURY DOOR KNOCKER   48

LIST OF ILLUSTRATIONS xi

		PAGE
Fig. 48.	Archaic Hammer of a XV Century Door Knocker	48
Fig. 49.	Door Knocker with a Single Bosse. Late XVI Century	46
Fig. 50.	Door Knocker with Double Bosse. Late XVI Century	46
Fig. 51.	Stirrup Knocker. XVII Century . .	48
Fig. 52.	Pilgrim Shell Knocker. Early XVII Century	48
Fig. 53.	One of a Pair of Gothic Door Knockers. XV Century	50
Fig. 54.	Door Knocker of Mudéjar Design. XVII Century	50
Fig. 55.	Knocker. Gothic in spirit but probably XVIII Century work	50
Fig. 56.	Door Knocker with Incised Patterning. XV Century	52
Fig. 57.	Ring Handle with Clinch. XVI Century	52
Fig. 58.	Ring Handle with Bosse. XVI Century	52
Fig. 59.	Ring Knocker of Moorish Inspiration. XVI Century	52
Fig. 60.	Ring Handle of Oriental Design. Late XVI Century	54
Fig. 61.	Door Knocker of Oriental Inspiration. About 1600	54

LIST OF ILLUSTRATIONS

Fig. 62. DOOR KNOCKER OF ORIENTAL DESIGN. Late XVI Century 54

Fig. 63. DOOR KNOCKER WITH MUDÉJAR TRACERY. Late XVI Century 56

Fig. 64. DOOR HANDLE WITH MUDÉJAR TRACERY. Late XVI Century 56

Fig. 65. DOOR KNOCKER WITH GOTHIC BACKPLATE. XVII Century 53

Fig. 66. GOTHIC KNOCKER. Late XVI Century 55

Fig. 67. RICH FLAMBOYANT KNOCKER. Middle XVI Century 58

Fig. 68. KNOCKER OF ARAGONESE TYPE. XVII Century 60

Fig. 69. KNOCKER OF ARAGONESE TYPE. XVII Century 60

Fig. 70. DOOR KNOCKER. Tentative Renaissance but made in the XVII Century 60

Fig. 71. DOOR KNOCKER WITH OPEN BACKPLATE. XVII Century 60

Fig. 72. DOOR KNOCKER OF EARLY RENAISSANCE DESIGN. About 1600 60

Fig. 73. CHEST LOCK WITH TYPICAL FIXING STAPLES. Late XV Century 62

Fig. 74. CHEST LOCK WITH CANOPY. Late XV Century 62

LIST OF ILLUSTRATIONS

	PAGE
Fig. 75. CHEST LOCK WITH FALSE FIXING STAPLE OVER KEYHOLE. Late XVI Century	58
Fig. 76. LOCK AND HASP. Elaborate Mudéjar design. XVII Century	64
Fig. 77. CHEST HASP. Late XVI Century	66
Fig. 78. CHEST HASP. Typical of the XVII Century	66
Fig. 79. CHEST HASP. Typical of the XVII Century	66
Fig. 80. LOCKPLATE AND HASP. Probably XVII Century	59
Fig. 81. ARCÓN, OR TRUNK WITH IRON FITTINGS	68
Fig. 82. SMALL LEATHER STRONG BOX	68
Fig. 83. TABLE CANDELERO PATTERNED AFTER THE ROMAN. In the Museum of Vich. XI Century	63
Fig. 84. TABLE CANDELERO. Catalan. In the Museum of Vich. XV Century	63
Fig. 85. ECCLESIASTICAL CANDELABRA. Catalan. In the Museum of Vich. XIII Century	64
Fig. 86. ECCLESIASTICAL CANDELABRA. Catalan. In the Museum of Vich. XV Century	64

LIST OF ILLUSTRATIONS

PAGE

Fig. 87. ECCLESIASTICAL CANDELABRA. XVI Century 68

Fig. 88. BRAZIER IN TWO STORIES. XVII Century 68

Fig. 89. BRAZIER ON WHEELS. Catalan. XIV Century 65

Fig. 90. IRON FIRE-DOG. Catalan. XV Century 66

Fig. 91. GUARD AND FIRE-DOGS. Museo del Greco, Toledo 67

Fig. 92. RENAISSANCE BAND IN REPOUSSÉ. Perforated. Early XVI Century . . . 70

Fig. 93. RENAISSANCE BAND IN REPOUSSÉ. XVI Century 70

Fig. 94. RENAISSANCE BAND IN REPOUSSÉ. Middle XVI Century 70

Fig. 95. RENAISSANCE BAND IN REPOUSSÉ. Late XVI Century 70

Fig. 96. NAVE OF BURGOS CATHEDRAL. Showing the importance of the reja in Spanish churches 72

Fig. 97. REJA OF THE CAPILLA DE SANTA LIBRADA. Sigüenza Cathedral. Early XVI Century 74

Fig. 98. REJA OF THE PUERTA DEL CARDO. León Cathedral. Late XV Century 76

LIST OF ILLUSTRATIONS

	PAGE
Fig. 99. Reja of the Capilla de Santa Magdalena. Cloisters of Tarragona Cathedral. Early XVI Century	76
Fig. 100. Reja of the Coro. Toledo Cathedral. 1549	76
Fig. 101. Reja of the Capilla Mayor. Sevilla Cathedral. 1518–33	78
Fig. 102. Panel of the Entombment. Reja of the Capilla Mayor, Sevilla Cathedral	87
Fig. 103. Reja of the Coro. Sevilla Cathedral. 1519	80
Fig. 104. Reja in the Capilla Real. Granada. 1523	82
Fig. 105. Arms of Ferdinand and Isabella and their Grandson Charles V. Reja in the Capilla Real, Granada. 1523	84
Fig. 106. Reja of the Capilla de la Presentación. Burgos Cathedral. Middle XVI Century	84
Fig. 107. Reja of the Capilla del Condestable. Burgos Cathedral. 1523	86
Fig. 108. Escalera Dorada or Golden Stairway. Burgos Cathedral. 1519	88
Fig. 109. Reja of the Coro. Palencia Cathedral. Probably 1555	90
Fig. 110. Reja of a Side Chapel. Cuenca Cathedral. Middle XVI Century	92

LIST OF ILLUSTRATIONS

	PAGE
Fig. 111. REJA OF A SIDE CHAPEL. Segovia Cathedral. Late XVI Century	92
Fig. 112. REJA OF THE CORO. Plasencia Cathedral, 1604	94
Fig. 113. PORTION OF A REJA CRESTING. Northern Spain. Early XVII Century.	96
Fig. 114. GATE REJA LEADING TO STAIRWAY. Salamanca University. Early XVI Century	98
Fig. 115. ENTRANCE REJA TO LIBRARY. Salamanca University. XVI Century	98
Fig. 116. ENTRANCE GATES. XVII Century	103
Fig. 117. TYPICAL FAÇADE WITH WINDOW REJAS. House in Granada	100
Fig. 118. WINDOW REJA, FAÇADE OF THE UNIVERSITY OF ALCALÁ	100
Fig. 119. WINDOW REJA, CASA DE PILATOS. Sevilla. Middle XVI Century	100
Fig. 120. WINDOW WITH REJA HOOD. Toledo. XVI Century	102
Fig. 121. WINDOW REJA. Façade of the Audiencia. Granada. XVII Century	106
Fig. 122. RENAISSANCE PULPIT. Avila Cathedral. Early XVI Century	104
Fig. 123. RENAISSANCE PULPIT. Sevilla Cathedral. Early XVI Century	106

LIST OF ILLUSTRATIONS

Fig. 124. SWINGING PULPIT. Monastery of Las Huelgas, Burgos. XVI Century . . . 106

Fig. 125. MOORISH KEYS. Sevilla Cathedral. Probably XII Century 110

Fig. 126. GOTHIC KEY, Aragonese. XIV Century 111

Fig. 127. SPANISH KEYS OF THE XVI, XVII, AND XVIII CENTURIES 108

Fig. 128. VARGUEÑO WITH DECORATIONS IN IRON. XVI Century 108

Fig. 129. FLATTENED OUT CORNER-BRACE OF A VARGUEÑO 114

Fig. 130. VARGUEÑO LOCK. XVI Century . . . 116

Fig. 131. FACE OF VARGUEÑO SHOWING IRON MOUNTINGS. XVI Century 110

Fig. 132. RUBBING FROM A VARGUEÑO LOCK-PLATE. XVI Century 114

Fig. 133. RUBBING FROM A VARGUEÑO LOCK-PLATE. XVII Century 114

Fig. 134. VARGUEÑO LOCKPLATE WITH HASP. XVII Century 116

Fig. 135. VARGUEÑO LOCKPLATE WITH HASP. XVII Century 116

Fig. 136. A PAIR OF RENAISSANCE FIXING-STAPLES 117

Fig. 137. A PAIR OF RENAISSANCE DOOR KNOCKERS. XVII Century 116

LIST OF ILLUSTRATIONS

	PAGE
Fig. 138. LOCKPLATE AND HASP. XVII Century	116
Fig. 139. KNOCKER EXHIBITING GREEK REVIVAL. XVIII Century	118
Fig. 140. DOOR KNOCKER. Renaissance backplate. Hammer of Classic Inspiration.	118
Fig. 141. DOOR HANDLE AND ESCUTCHEON PLATE. From a Palace in Palma, Balearic Isles. XVII Century	119
Fig. 142. BALCONY FRONT. From a Palace in Palma. XVIII Century	121
Fig. 143. BALCONY WITH A CURVED FRONT. Palace in Palma. XVIII Century	121
Figs. 144 and 145. BALCONIES WITH SCROLL BRACKETS. Salamanca. XVIII Century	120
Fig. 146. BALCONY WITH OVERHEAD BRACES. Santa Coloma de Queralt, Catalonia. Dated 1760	122
Fig. 147. IRON STAIR-BALUSTRADE. Patio of the Palacio Oleza. Palma	122
Fig. 148. ARMADURA OR WELL CRANE. Palma. XVII Century	122
Fig. 149. TYPICAL IRON BRACKET	123
Fig. 150. CRUZ DE LINDE OR BOUNDARY CROSS. Catalan. XV Century	124
Fig. 151. TABLE WITH WROUGHT IRON BRACES.	126

LIST OF ILLUSTRATIONS xix

Fig. 152. ONE OF FOUR IRON CHAIRS OF THE XVII CENTURY 127

Fig. 153. CATALAN GRIDIRON. XVII Century . 128

Fig. 154. SPANISH BIT WITH ORNAMENTS TO WARD OFF THE EVIL EYE. XVII Century 126

Fig. 155. SPUR OF A CONQUISTADOR. XVI Century 126

Fig. 156. STIRRUP OF A CONQUISTADOR. XVI Century 126

Fig. 157. GRILLE IN MARKET, Granada. Late XVIII Century 128

Fig. 158. DOOR IRONWORK OF THE CASA CONSISTORIAL. Barcelona. Late XIX Century 128

INTRODUCTION

SPAIN is rich in decorative ironwork which, like the architecture it embellishes, is comparatively unknown. Of the two arts it is Spanish ironwork that owes least to foreign influence, for those who practised it were, in contrast to the many foreign architects employed, almost invariably native born. Little is known of individual workers of the Gothic age; from the Renaissance period, however, a few names have come down to us but without those intimate details which make the craftsman a living and present reality to the modern who admires his work. To appreciate the productions of these unrecorded artists one must know something of metalwork in general as practised in the East, since to iron the Spanish Moors imparted, along with their basic principles of design, their delicate methods of working gold and silver; one must be familiar also with French ironwork during the Romanesque and early Gothic periods, for that, too, influenced the Spanish smith; and lastly, one must understand Renaissance architecture as evolved in Italy because that style, when it came to Spain, so stimulated the ironworker that he attained an amazing grandeur and architectonic quality in his work that was never approached elsewhere. In Italy itself, ironworking was not a popular craft; it was rather on the precious metals that great artists like Benvenuto Cellini expended their talent; but in Spain the baser and less tractable metal appealed more to the indomitable temper of the people, and artists of the highest rank worked in it. These, apprehending that its inherent quality, strength, was best expressed on a grand scale, created those monumental works which give Spain a unique position in the realm of artistic ironwork.

Outside of the country itself it is hardly possible to study these achievements, since their size and weight have made removal practically impossible; but there, still standing in the very surroundings for which they were designed, they make a journey to Spain well worth while for the student.

Monumentality is but one of the distinguishing features of Spanish ironwork; an equally interesting one is that exotic feeling which pervades all the industrial arts, and even the architecture, of Spain. The Moorish occupation of seven centuries is a circumstance unparalleled in any other European country and its influence on all Spanish art was lasting. This Orientalism, sometimes preserved pure, sometimes combined with European designs, is to be found mostly in smaller objects, and may therefore be studied in the various museums which have succeeded in obtaining examples. Larger Mudéjar productions, such as the grand doors at Córdova, being as difficult of transportation as the great church rejas, must remain unknown to many except through photographs and description.

As is natural in a country where inspiration has so frequently been drawn from foreign sources, there is a certain lack of continuity in the development of the various arts, not excluding ironwork. This, while sometimes baffling, never fails to be interesting. Fortunately, foreign influence never undermined the Spanish smith's reverence for sound constructive methods; these prevailed to the end and lend a certain sincerity to even the latest period when the frankness and naïveté of early work had been lost.

CELTIBERIAN SWORD.

Found at Amarejo.
Hispanic Society of America.
No. 161.

SPANISH IRONWORK

I

SPANISH IRONWORK PREVIOUS TO THE GOTHIC PERIOD

EARLY PRODUCTIONS

SPAIN was the greatest metalliferous country of antiquity, but history fails to tell us at what period the use and manufacture of iron was first known there. There is every evidence, as in other European countries, of a native industry in copper and silver, and of a knowledge of bronze, before iron was discovered. In connection with it, one of the earliest facts known is that the Greek colonists who settled Marseilles in the sixth century B.C. operated iron mines in Spain, from which they fashioned their war weapons. After the Spanish people came under Roman rule they used those types of Roman arms and utensils found in every elementary book on archeology; there was, however, one exception to the general rule of the conqueror imposing his tools on the conquered, and this was the Celtiberian sword, which the invaders found so superior to their own that it was adopted for the Roman army after the Second Punic War. These swords were unusually wide and could cut on both edges; one found at Amarejo may be seen in the Hispanic Society's collection, No. 161. The Romans, when they began to manufacture them, were not able to imitate the excellent manner of their tempering, but later acquired great skill in sword making, especially in Bilbilis (the modern Calatayud in the province of Aragon).

Of the earliest iron weapons and domestic utensils, which latter were probably made of very crudely smelted metal, hardly an example has survived. From Visigothic days, the fifth to the eighth century, we have even less data on the manufacture and use of iron. It appears that these next conquerors modified its use in armor considerably, doing away with the iron breastplates and protective leg pieces of the Romans. When, in the eighth century, the Moors took possession, they imported their own special arms and weapons, copied for the most part from the Persians. As for other objects than war implements, it is probable that few were produced, for the Moors preferred the more precious metals, bronze above all. Spanish Christians, meanwhile, were using the same armor as other European states, and were ordering it from those northern provinces of the peninsula which the Moors never succeeded in conquering. It frequently happens that objects from this period are classified as French from their likeness to work produced on the other side of the Pyrenees.

It was in the progressive northern region of Catalonia that the best type of early forge for smelting iron was evolved. This was the Catalan forge (Figure 1)

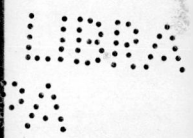

FIG. 2. SANTA CRUZ REJA.
Pamplona Cathedral.   Early XIII Century.

EASTON PUBLIC LIBRARY
EASTON PA

PREVIOUS TO THE GOTHIC PERIOD 3

which may still be met with in remote parts of Europe. From it was obtained the best malleable iron yet

FIG. 1. EARLY CATALAN FORGE.

known, easily wrought, free from foreign matter and bubbles, and in large enough quantities to be available for the forging of truly artistic works. It is therefore to the provinces north of the Ebro that we must look for the earliest and best specimens of Spanish decorative iron.

Previous to the Catalan forge the only means of smelting iron was the open hearth fire used as far back as early Egyptian days and still used in certain parts of India by native smiths. This most primitive metallurgical contrivance was a mere basin-shaped hollow in the ground containing ignited charcoal and the substances to be smelted; the fire was urged by a blast of air blown in through one or more nozzles from a bellows at or near the top. The process gave but a small amount of metal and consumed a large amount of charcoal. What the Catalans devised was a rectangular hearth in a permanent building close to the mine. The square pit was lined with brick or stone of a kind not easily acted upon by heat, and was supplied with a tuyère or blast-pipe of copper penetrating one of the pit walls near the top. This tuyère had a considerable downward inclination so that the air met the fuel some distance down. In iron-smelting, the ore was laid in a heap upon an eighteen-inch layer of charcoal and was gradually brought to the metallic state by the reducing action of the carbon monoxide formed at the mouth of the tuyère. The metal sank through the ignited fuel and formed at the bottom of the pit a spongy mass or bloom which was lifted over the edge and carried to the nearby forge. A mere hole in the roof of the building served as a chimney.

How imperfect this newer process was is proven by the fact that thousands of tons of slag from the Catalan forge have since been profitably smelted. Yet it was such an advance on what had preceded it that it was installed all over Europe (perhaps in Germany and Belgium simultaneously with Catalonia) and remained for centuries the best thing of its kind. By yielding

FIG. 3. REJA ARABE, CAPILLA DEL SAGRARIO.
Palencia Cathedral.   XIII Century.

EASTON PUBLIC LIBRARY
EASTON PA

FIG. 4. WINDOW REJA.
Nuestra Señora Del Mercado, León.
Late XIII Century.

EASTON PUBLIC LIBRARY
EASTON PA

an excellent malleable iron it made possible the great quantity of beautiful medieval ironwork.

Malleable iron may be described as that which is capable of being welded; it becomes steel when hardened by tempering until it strikes sparks from flint. Cast iron is that which can neither be hammered nor welded. Malleable iron has at first a granulated texture but becomes, through repeated heatings, hammerings, and rollings, quite tough and flexible, and its granulated texture changes into a fibrous and interwoven one. Besides being easily wrought when hot, it may be hammered and bent when cold. Tempering it in cold water renders it slightly harder, while hammering, drawing, and other such processes make it both harder and more elastic. If reheated and allowed to cool gradually, it becomes soft and weldable again (for which reason much beautiful early iron was remade into later, and perhaps inferior, forms). During heating it passes through various grades of workability as the temperature increases, first becoming red-hot, then white-hot. It is in this latter condition that it may be bent, stretched, or welded with greatest ease.

"The texture of iron, it is well known, becomes loosened by heat; and as it softens, bars will droop and curl into scrolls under a relatively slight impulse, this property rendering it so facile a metal in the hands of the smith. When hot it can be welded, separate pieces adhering firmly together if hammered or pressed; rich and intricate effects were mainly produced in this manner. The welding point is the highest degree of heat the iron will bear without burning and disintegrating, and its management requires skill and dexterity. The distinction between the blacksmith's art and any other is that whatever he intends to do he must do quickly. He must strike while the iron is hot, for as the fierce glow fades into dull red its plasticity is departing. The quick and decisive treatment of iron while it is hot and transiently in a plastic condition must be regarded as the true art of the blacksmith, and of necessity leads to vigorous and masculine efforts. The tools of the smithy proper consist merely of hammer and anvil, forge and bellows, tongs and chisels. In the work to be described, small objects, however complicated in design, were nearly always welded into a single piece; while in grilles, the several pieces were fixed by driving holes through the heated iron and riveting them together, or more commonly by binding the pieces round with hot wisps of iron called collars.

"In appreciating old work we must not forget that, while the smith of to-day can buy his iron ready rolled into a thousand different sections, he had then to first beat out every section with his own hand. Hence old ironwork possesses interest and attractions which few modern examples can equal, for scarcely any old piece fails to please. The explanation is simply that the olden-time smith cut a piece from his shingled bar which he judged by the eye would beat out into a rod of the desired length or curl into a scroll of the desired form. More or less sufficed for him, and by his method of work he produced an irregularity and play in even the most monotonous designs, which is artistically charming to us, but which was possibly a source of reproach to

FIG. 7. DETACHED NAILHEADS OR BOSSES.
XVI Century.
Hispanic Society of America.
Average 4 in. sq.   Nos. 40, 42, 43, 46, 6, 7.

EASTON PUBLIC LIBRARY
EASTON PA

himself. The designs are so practical, yet so rude, that they were probably produced by the smith who executed the work. Even if directed by a designer, the smith's capacity must have been thoroughly gauged, and the technical details left well within his powers. It appears that, when no specially skilled smith was available, only the simplest forms were used, the capacity of the workers controlling the demand." J. Starkie Gardner.

For centuries the laborious task of fashioning the desired object direct from the bloom fell to the smith as described above; there were no mechanical aids to lessen his work. Later the helve hammer was installed weighing from twelve hundred to twenty-four hundred pounds, and worked by a rough cog-wheel driven by water power. This hammer beat and rebeat the bloom into manageable units or ingots, which could be transported and delivered to the smith, thus making it possible for him to live at a distance from the mines. Mechanical hammering dates from perhaps the fourteenth century; and until the seventeenth century, the bars or ingots that it prepared for the smith were not fit to be used for fine work until the bestowal of much labor upon them.

About the lost art of treating iron so as to reduce rusting to a minimum, there has been much speculation. It is generally believed that the result was obtained by oil dipping; that is, by heating the metal to a brilliant cherry red and thus separating the molecules, and then immediately immersing it in linseed or any fine, transparent oil, which entered the spongy mass to perhaps only an imperceptible depth, yet sufficient to ward off rust, and to create a superficial hardness which made such iron available for tools; furthermore, it gave a surface which could be brought to a fairly high polish. Certain it is that modern exposed ironwork, unless protected by successive coats of paint which rob it of all its inherent attractiveness of surface, will deteriorate almost to powder in a century or even less.

ROMANESQUE REJAS

Decorative ironwork everywhere followed the various styles of architecture; and as Spain (that is, northern Spain where the smith was most important) had no definite style of architecture until Romanesque was introduced from France, the story of Spanish iron does not really commence until Romanesque had firmly taken root in the land. Previous to its appearance the remnant of the Visigoths whom the Moors had driven into the upper peninsular had been too hard pressed, first with the mere struggle for existence and later in the struggle to push back the invader, to give heed to the arts; but with their first important victories over the Moors, in the eleventh century, their gratitude was expressed in church-building. As, at this time, Spanish kings were accustomed to taking French wives, who brought with them their own retinues of monks of the great building order of Cluny, these erected the new Spanish churches in the French Romanesque style.

Romanesque was not conspicuous, as its successor Gothic became, for the use of ironwork; but, happening to make its first appearance in those Spanish provinces, the Pyrenean and Cantabrian, where iron was more plentiful and wood more scarce than in France, the Cluniac builders learned to use it quite freely as an accessory in their Romanesque edifices. One of the first demands they made on the Spanish smith was for a reja,[1] or screen, to protect the treasures of the altar. Tracing the history of the screen we find that metal ones of simple design were made by the Romans. Several later examples have been found in sixth and seventh century Christian basilicas; but those necessitated to protect the more precious offerings and reliquaries of medieval cathedrals are on a much larger scale. Their motif is invariably the scroll derived from the vine which had been so highly conventionalized in Greek and Roman art. The ease with which a bar of iron could be made to take the scroll form would, in itself, explain why this preponderated as a decorative motif in early smithing; the very anvil was made to produce scrolls, for it was shaped to a peak or ridge over which the red hot bar could be bent by blows. When other methods than genuine smithing crept in — that is, when the metal was worked cold by tools formerly associated with other crafts — the scroll became a much less frequent element. The St. Swithin grille of Winchester Cathedral in England, one at Le Puy-en-Velay in France and several in Spain show in what widely separated localities this type was popular during the Middle Ages. That the examples mentioned have remained *in situ* during all these centuries is due not

[1] Pronounced raý-hah.

only to their size and durability but also to the fact that they are serving their original purpose of protecting altars still open to the cult. One of the best known of the type is in the cathedral cloister in Pamplona, the capital of Navarre.

The little Santa Cruz chapel at Pamplona occupies the southwest corner of the cloisters in such a way that two of its sides are masonry and two are open to the cloister. Both these latter are protected by the famous grille, a portion of which is shown in Figure 2. In the scrolls, some loosely wound and others wrapped into a dense whorl, there is infinite variety; likewise in the manner of strapping the scroll units back to back, some being augmented by short strips before being tied in, others connected by a loose filigree. In addition, occasional leaf forms and tendrils are seen which further prevent the scroll from becoming monotonous and lend a degree of interest which makes the Spanish example superior to contemporaneous French or English ones. A peculiarity which further distinguishes the Pamplona work is that the scrolls do not terminate in perfect rings, but stop abruptly, leaving the end of the whorl without any decorative finish whatever. The liliaceous cresting of the Pamplona reja is of later date. Whether its scroll pattern was borrowed from France or England would be difficult to say. The Pamplona grille, though not dated, is supposed to have been made out of Moorish tent chains captured by the Navarrese in 1212, and may therefor be ascribed to the early thirteenth century; but the English example at Winchester dates from 1093; so that Spain, while she may

FIG. 9. IRON-MOUNTED DOOR.
Avila.
Early XVI Century.

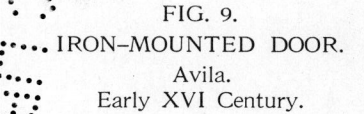

FIG. 8.
BOSSES AND KNOCKERS.
Count of Toledo's house.
XVI Century.

not have imported the design, cannot claim to have been the first to use it.

At Palencia, in the cathedral, there is the so-called Reja Arabe de la Capilla del Sagrario (Figure 3). It is a beautiful example, similar to the Pamplona, but less naïve. Its various scrolls are more like each other in size and treatment, indicating a later date. The frame to which these scrolls were originally riveted having deteriorated, is now replaced by stout wood. This same sort of Romanesque grille may be found in León. Here, however, it is acting as a window screen on the façade of Nuestra Señora del Mercado (Figure 4). This little example is only thirty inches wide and four feet, six inches high. Vertically the design is divided into three panels, with the scrolls worked into such a number of whorls that the pattern becomes very dense, not unlike Venetian point lace. An interesting detail here is the little tendrils which spring from between the scrolls. This grille may be placed, judging from the symmetry of the pattern, at the end of the thirteenth century. San Vicente in Avila, a Romanesque church commenced in the twelfth century, also possesses a bit of this work and undoubtedly many more once existed than are here mentioned, but they have disintegrated or been broken up.

Of small iron objects belonging to this period not many have survived, and these can be found only in collections. The richest collection open to the public is that of the Episcopal Museum of Vich, a town in northern Catalonia. Vich Museum owes its existence to a recent art-loving bishop who, noting with regret that all too many of Spain's treasures were being sold to foreigners, scoured his province to save what he could. His search resulted in the assembling, at Vich, of a remarkable display of Catalonian painting, sculpture, embroidery, and ironwork, a fair amount of the last-named dating from the thirteenth century. A few pieces are illustrated later in this book.

MOORISH INFLUENCE

While the forged ironwork already referred to was being produced north of the Ebro, that produced in Castile and Andalucía was affected by the presence of Moorish artizans working in other metals. In fact, of all foreign influences, the Arab taste played the most important part. The Saracens, when they crossed from Africa into Spain, brought with them no truly structural architecture nor did they subsequently create one. They were, and ever remained, supreme ornamentalists, and in this direction their ingenuity was unbounded. Of their ornament may be said that which is not true of their architecture — that it was structural. It differed from the usual Asiatic conception in that it was not made up of graceful natural forms but of logically combined geometric patterns. That this Moorish taste persisted even after the Reconquest is due to the fact that the Spaniard, recognizing the superior craftsmanship of the Moor, employed him side by side with the Spanish artizans whenever Christian buildings were to be erected. Each may have learned from the other, though unquestionably it was the Moor who had most to teach. By degrees Moorish

FIG. 10. COPPER-PLATED DOORS.
Puerta del Perdón, Mosque of Córdova. 1377.

EASTON PUBLIC LIBRARY
EASTON PA

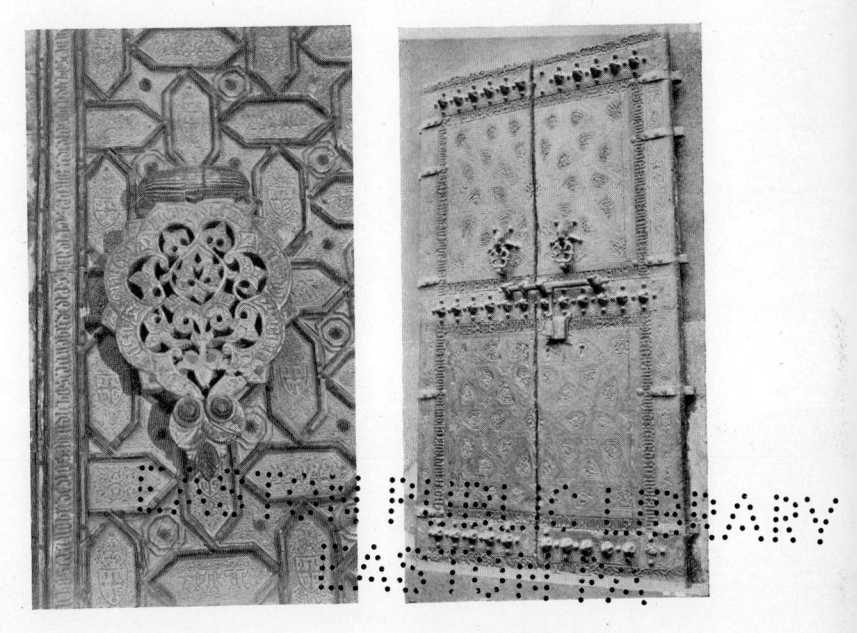

FIG. 11.
DETAILS OF PANELING
AND KNOCKER.
Puerta del Perdón.

FIG. 12.
BRONZE-MOUNTED DOORS.
From Sevilla Cathedral, now in the
Museo Nacional, Madrid.
Late XIV Century.

EASTON PUBLIC LIBRARY
EASTON PA

and Gothic art were blended into what is called Mudéjar, and as geometric forms were the basis of each, the result was particularly harmonious. Neither in architecture nor in ornament could Mudéjar be called a new style; it is simply a curiously happy application of elements ordinarily incongruous to whatever style of structure happened to be in progress.

It must not be inferred that Spain was the only European country to receive Oriental influences in art. Italy, France and England were also affected; but the difference is that to them the new ideas came less directly, their princes having definitely set about modifying the rude European civilization by cultivating the Eastern refinement they had seen during the Crusades. Saracenic art and architecture, answering this demand, penetrated into Western Europe by following the trade routes, principally that of Venice whence it passed into other states. In Venice itself may be found the earliest decorative ironwork in Italy — a few grilles copying the pierced marble screens used so extensively in Saracenic architecture. Spain, however, did not have to get her Eastern art in this roundabout way. The Saracen was there, on her soil, and as he was a cunning craftsman, and as the Spaniard himself had no liking for the humbler callings, the matter of erecting and ornamenting buildings was left largely in the hands of the Moors.

When, occasionally, the Arab used iron it was worked as were the more precious metals, with file and saw, vice and drill, instead of being subjected only to the powerful blows of the smith's hammer; in other words,

14   PREVIOUS TO THE GOTHIC PERIOD

the Moor had no conception of pure smithing, for which reason an early piece of Castilian or Andalucian ironwork would be easily distinguishable from a contemporaneous piece wrought in Catalonia or Navarre. Iron was never really popular, however, until its use as a decorative architectural feature spread from England and France down into Spain, creating great demand even among the Moors for this hitherto neglected metal. Spain, indeed, carried its use farther than did the countries north of the Pyrenees. Door hardware, with the exception of the strap hinge, developed to a point undreamed of elsewhere; knockers, escutcheons, bosses being infinitely more plentiful. Hardly a window in the land but had an iron grille or reja, for window screening, universal with the Moors, had been copied from them by the Spaniards. When furniture came into general use (early Spanish houses were as devoid of chairs and tables as Moorish homes were) iron was often used as a diagonal brace between vertical supports, and even entire chairs, tables, etc., were made of it. When in due time the balcony began to be an architectural feature it was upheld by a row of interesting scroll brackets. In the churches, candelabra became massive and imposing, railings or screens (verjas) surrounded tombs, chapel rejas grew to be of towering height, and even entire pulpits were beaten out of iron. Much of this work is Mudéjar.

ORNAMENTAL NAILHEADS

One of the most familiar Moorish inheritances, although a minor one, is the decorative nailhead, known

FIG. 13. IRON-PLATED DOORS.
Main Portal of Tarragona Cathedral. 1510.

PREVIOUS TO THE GOTHIC PERIOD 15

as a *chatón*. Introduced by the Moors, it persisted down to Spain's last decorative moment, and instantly marks any object bearing it as Spanish. The first examples found are solid, slightly accentuated heads of otherwise ordinary nails which are part of door construction. Two such nails from a door in the Alhambra are shown in Figure 5, and two others from a Spanish building in Figure 6. In the making of rejas the head

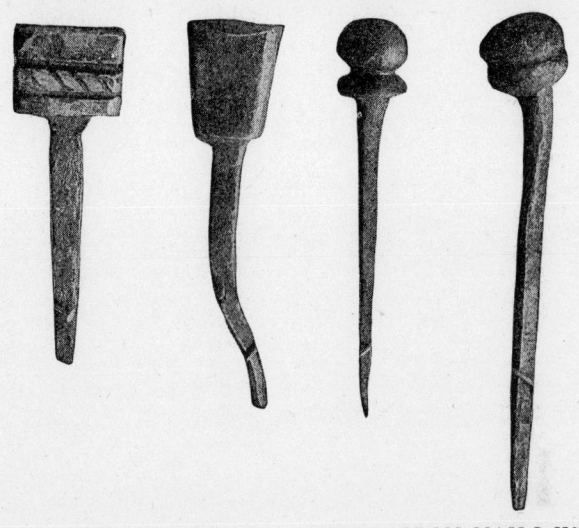

FIG. 5. IRON NAILS WITH WROUGHT HEADS.
Moorish.   XIV Century.
Hispanic Society of America.
Length 4 and 5 in.   Nos. 13, 14.

FIG. 6. IRON NAILS WITH WROUGHT HEADS.
Spanish.   XVI Century.
Hispanic Society of America.
Length 5 and 7 in.   Nos. 27, 28.

of a rivet was similarly treated. As the nail grew in size and ornamentation, to hammer it into place became difficult and the head was therefore made separately (Figure 7) while the nail, often of great size, was driven through afterwards. In many of the largest, however, the nail or stem remained an integral part of the decorative head and was split and passed through a hole bored in the door, and then spread on the inside. Once the nailhead became a separate unit, there was no limit to the freshness of fancy shown in its making; sometimes it was convex, sometimes flat; slashed towards the center and with scalloped edges; or the center sunk into a hollow to receive the nail, while the remaining portion was beaten out from the back into a large bosse. These various results arrived at while the metal was hot, further enrichment such as chasing and piercing was added when it became cold. In short, the nailhead or bosse soon outgrew its original utilitarian function and became primarily ornamental. It is seen employed singly over an entire door surface or in groups of three, five or seven. Applied thus it made a metal door decoration vastly different to the strap hinges used elsewhere in Europe. It is sometimes stated that the Visigoths of Toledo also used bosses — an erroneous impression derived from the number of late Mudéjar palace entrances in that city reconstructed out of Visigothic stone fragments; the actual wooden doors, however, are invariably remnants of the Moorish or even of the Reconquest period, and were made for Christian masters by Moorish workmen. Two late doors are illustrated (Figures 8 and 9), one from Toledo and the other from Avila, which give an excellent idea of the Spanish preference for these bosses. It is to be regretted that many of those on the Toledo example have recently been sold separately to tourists.

FIG. 14. CLOISTER REJAS.
Barcelona Cathedral. Early XIV Century.

EASTON PUBLIC LIBRARY
EASTON PA

PREVIOUS TO THE GOTHIC PERIOD

MUDÉJAR METAL DOORS

Returning to general Moorish ironwork, not enough smaller objects remain to dwell upon; but certain bronze and copper doors may be described here since they served as prototypes for later iron-plated ones. In the Mosque of Córdova, still in their original position, are the great copper-plated doors of the Puerta del Perdon (Figures 10 and 11). They were made by Moors, but after the Reconquest; and as the date (1377), Gothic inscriptions, and saints all prove, were ordered by Christians. The patterning here — typical Saracenic geometric patterning — has been cut from sheet metal and superimposed upon another sheet or background, a form of decoration to be met later in Gothic ironwork. The copper knockers, on the contrary, are not of sheet metal, but of solid copper apparently worked in the mass as iron would have been. In design these recall the Byzantine stone screens seen in Venice and Ravenna; but the bronze paneling of the doors is distinctly Saracenic. Figure 12 illustrates a pair of bronze mounted wooden doors now in the Museo-Nacional of Madrid. Here the decoration is entirely Moorish, but the doors, as the Gothic lettering shows, were destined for Christian use and long served for the Sacristy of the High Altar of Sevilla Cathedral. The all-over patterning is incised in the wood, the star being the foundation of the scheme. Across the top, bottom, and center of the doors broad metal bands are riveted. These are worked into an interesting circular pattern in low relief, and are held down by large and small ornamental nailheads arranged to accommodate the design. The bronze knocker with a star-shaped backplate and each point of the star finished off in a knob, may have inspired the maker of Figure 59, which is in iron. Bolts like that of the Madrid bronze example are found on many later doors and grilles.

Of iron-covered doors, one of the earliest pieces, standing, as the English architect George Street describes it "in a monumental recess of completely Moorish character," is in the cloister of Tarragona Cathedral. It may be classed as thirteenth century work and is of wood once completely covered by iron plates which were stamped and gilded and fastened down with copper nails. Later by nearly three centuries, but still designed in the Moorish taste, are the colossal, iron-plated main doors of the famous west façade of this same cathedral (Figure 13). These were presented to the chapter in 1510 by Archbishop Gonzalo de Heredia. Their enormous height is apparent on comparing them with the children playing at their base. These doors are of wood covered by many diapered iron plates fastened down with copper nails, and with a copper rosette in the center of each plate. Hinges and knockers are most elaborate in design. In the back plates of the knockers and in the huge hinges at the top a very decorative result is obtained by successive thicknesses of pierced tracery, a Moorish idea already illustrated in Figure 12. Indeed, the whole scheme with its flat patterning broken up only by the shadow of the knockers, is thoroughly Oriental. Of these last adjuncts, the upper and more elaborate is obviously

FIG. 15. REJA OF A CLOISTER CHAPEL.
Barcelona Cathedral.

EASTON PUBLIC LIBRARY
EASTON PA

too high for the human arm and was undoubtedly applied merely as a matter of tradition. Other notable doors are in the west portal of Santa Maria del Mar at Barcelona and in the main portal of Huesca Cathedral. The former are covered with iron plates cut to a pattern, and the latter with beaten iron which is fastened down with nails whose heads appear to be brass.

II
GOTHIC REJAS AND PULPITS
EARLY CHAPEL REJAS

IN the thirteenth century King Fernando III (El Santo) introduced French Gothic by ordering the magnificent cathedrals of Burgos, Toledo, and León to be built. Catalonia, though remote from these centers, was not slow to adopt the new style and developed under native architects many features that differentiated it from the parent stock. Such, for instance, were the wide naves and widely spaced piers of Gerona, Manresa, and Barcelona cathedrals. Of these distinctive edifices Barcelona is richest in ironwork and this of a sufficiently original character to be considered entirely as a Spanish product.

As the new style of architecture demanded a much more plentiful use of iron accessories than Romanesque had, great impetus was given to the smith's art. The response was at first all in the field of genuine blacksmithing quite unaffected by Moorish methods which did not appear north of the Ebro until later. By the fourteenth century the smiths' guilds had grown very important in Pamplona, Barcelona and other towns. The most important Gothic product was, as in Romanesque days, the reja, but it was of an entirely new design in which scrolls played no part; for the rejeros (reja-makers) decided that a number of spaced ver-

FIG. 16. REJA OF A CLOISTER CHAPEL.
Barcelona Cathedral.

EASTON PUBLIC LIBRARY
EASTON PA

FIG. 20. WINDOW REJA. Casa de las Conchas, Salamanca. 1514.

FIG. 19. WINDOW REJA. Archiepiscopal Palace, Salamanca. XVI Century.

tical bars, strengthened top and bottom and at some intermediate point by horizontals, would answer their purpose better than the all-over scroll pattern. That is, upright bars, by allowing no convenient horizontal footholds, would afford more protection to the sacred treasures in the chapel and at the same time render them more visible to worshippers. The increased openness of the new design is instantly apparent; likewise its increased architectonic quality, for its assertive verticality made it a most harmonious accessory to the dominating lines of Gothic architecture. The bar type therefor became the accepted convention in Spain, and was developed to a point undreamed of in other countries. The only thing of the kind in France is a simple and not very high grille in the church of St. Sernin in Toulouse; but this, according to Viollet-le-Duc, was made at least fifty years later than the earliest Barcelona example. Besides the greater loftiness of the Barcelona work, there is a structural peculiarity important to note as opposed to the French example in Toulouse; namely, that in early Gothic Spain an overwhelming partiality was shown for the round instead of the square bar; and that when the square bar was later accepted, it was invariably placed on the diagonal so that instead of one, two of its faces were visible. Indeed, in even the earliest Spanish rejas, many features may be met that already indicate the admirable originality and grandeur of those sixteenth century examples which have made the Spanish rejero so renowned.

Than the Barcelona cloisters, now a charming public

thoroughfare, no one spot in Spain offers a more favorable opportunity for studying the round-bar reja. A succession of twenty chapels borders three sides of the enclosure, each chapel screened off by a reja. These examples, though of varying heights, harmonize so well with each other and with their surroundings, that one might suspect their design of having been controlled by the architect of the cathedral. However, at this period the blacksmith was so highly important that it is safe to say that he needed no such control. This ensemble of ironwork may be considered the finest of its period in Europe.

The bar type naturally precluded ornamentation from the body of the reja, and left it for the cresting, the gates, and the lock. In certain of the Barcelona group (Figure 14) the actual gate or entrance to the chapel can hardly be detected; in others it is decidedly accentuated by means of Gothic arches ornamented by crocketed pinnacles. Where the entire door is framed in Gothic forms, these are set well forward of the bars, or else applied in such a way as not to interfere with the general structurability of the design (Figures 15 and 16), a rule violated with less pleasing results in later days. Horizontals are sparingly used, and toward the top only, the lower ends of the bars being embedded in the stone base and not further braced by a cross member. On the horizontal bar at each interval where the vertical round bar is threaded through, may be seen a bulge; the early smith after making the hole with his crude tools never felt it necessary to remove this evidence of the operation, or else

FIG. 21. LATTICE REJA.
Puerta del Obispo Tenorio, Cloisters of
Toledo Cathedral.
Circa 1400.

FIG. 22. LATTICE WINDOW
REJA.
House of Pedro Davila, Avila.
XVI Century.

EASTON PUBLIC LIBRARY
EASTON PA

GOTHIC REJAS AND PULPITS

had no tools adequate. It is just such interesting touches that one misses in later and more sophisticated work. In even the severest Barcelona rejas there is a decorative termination above, too rudimentary perhaps to be called a cresting since it consists of nothing more than finishing every third or fourth rod with a foliated picket. In others, however, the termination is really imposing — a row of tall liliaceous forms curled and twisted together. Beneath this may

FIG. 17. DETAIL OF REJA LOCK.
Cloister Chapel, Barcelona Cathedral.

be seen sometimes a broad ornamental band, sometimes a row of cusped arches set forward of the general plane (Figure 16).

Pamplona, the capital of Navarre, has been mentioned as another great ironworking center of Romanesque and Gothic days. However, between its scroll-shaped example of the thirteenth century and its several bar type examples, there is a long interval, for the last mentioned are later than the Barcelona work just described. The *capilla mayor* (high altar) reja is the best known of the Pamplona group. Its body is composed of alternating plain and twisted square verticals — an arrangement that remained popular in Spain till the end of its ironwork life. The bars are set close together and are devoid of all ornament, but, as George Street says in his *Gothic Architecture in Spain*, "What the lower part lacks in ornament the cresting more than atones for; it is unusually rich, consisting of interlacing ogee arches with crocketed

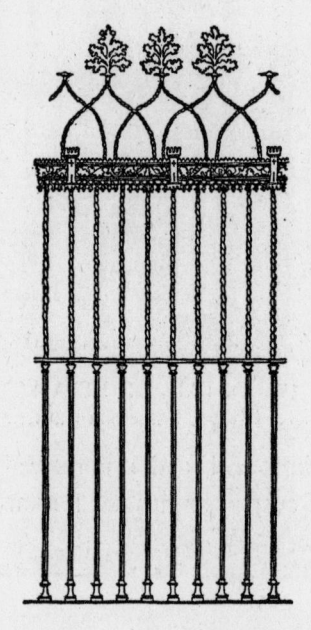

FIG. 18. REJA, CAPILLA DE NUESTRA SEÑORA DE LAS ANGUSTIAS.
Church of San Pablo, Palencia. Early XV Century.

FIG. 25. SPLIT BAR MOTIF.
Reja of the Royal Chapel, Granada. 1518–23.

pinnacles between them, all very elaborately hammered up. The horizontal bars and rails are also covered with traceries in relief and at regular intervals on these are small figures under canopies. The whole stands upon a moulded and paneled base of stone. The total height of this screen is not less than thirty feet, of which the cresting is about a third." This appearance of extensive figure work in iron modeled entirely out of the solid is interesting to note in view of the fact that it was later developed to an amazing point of skill.

In Palencia, another town which contributed much to early ironwork, is the Gothic reja of the Capilla de Nuestra Señora de las Angustias in the church of San Pablo (Figure 18). Dating from the early fifteenth century it is of simple design, with rather thin bars set far apart, as in much early work. Over the whole there is a tentative cresting composed of interlaced twisted rods in the form of pointed arches. This reja is so ingeniously wrought and of such an interesting period that its present state of unrepair is particularly lamentable. The little blazon and the amorini in the center were added in Renaissance days.

WINDOW REJAS

Most ubiquitous, possibly of all iron architectural accessories in Spain is the window reja. Brought over by the Moors it is still much in evidence in old Moorish cities like Toledo, Granada, Sevilla, etc. The following passage from the ordinances of Granada for the year 1522 may serve to show how numerous were rejas in that recently acquired Moorish city. "Whereas we have witnessed and do witness daily numerous mishaps to wayfarers alike on horseback and on foot whether by day or by night because the highways, narrow in themselves, are rendered yet more narrow by projecting rejas, fixed in basements and lower rooms of houses; and whereas in winter people seeking to escape the filth by keeping to the wall are thwarted, or at night injured, it is ordered that no rejas be set within three yards of the ground or else that they be set within the wall." In the ancient Castilian city of Toro, which was much earlier wrested from the Moors, hardly a handful of people have lived for centuries past and the city fathers have received no complaints from injured pedestrians; therefore there may still be seen a number of rejas sweeping the very ground and projecting a considerable distance from the façades.

Even where security would not have demanded a grating, the window was barred apparently through sheer love of the custom, though the Spaniard insists that the iron takes up the sun's heat and thus keeps it from entering the room. The original eastern screen was of wood or reed in a sort of basket or lattice weave, usually on the diagonal. At first there was some attempt to reproduce this in iron by means of strips interlaced or else riveted together at every intersection; but the smith soon abandoned this idea for the greater architectural possibilities of the vertical bar. One very close reproduction of a wooden lattice may still be seen in Toledo on an ancient palace near the

FIG. 27. GOTICO-FLORIDO REJA.
Casa de las Conchas, Salamanca. 1514.

FIG. 28. GOTICO-FLORIDO REJA.
Casa de las Conchas, Salamanca. 1514.

EASTON PUBLIC LIBRARY
EASTON PA

Alcázar. It is eight feet high, projects about two feet, and is divided into a number of panels, each treated differently, but always with small interstices specially intended to screen the inmates of the house from public gaze. Of the diagonal variety, two examples from Salamanca are shown (Figures 19 and 20). These are not particularly early, both being on noted Renaissance edifices. Their construction is simplicity itself, all the bars of one direction passing through their opposites. In one case, the Archiepiscopal Palace, there is a combination of diagonals with vertical bars above; in the other, the Casa de las Conchas, rosettes border the entire edge of the reja. For windows as unpretentious as these, the lattice grille is unquestionably of more domestic aspect than unadorned vertical bars of heavier section which, when not used on a monumental scale, savor too much of the prison. A glance at Figure 19, where one type occurs above the other, will justify the comparison. The cloisters of Toledo Cathedral contain an earlier example of diagonal lattice work made probably about 1400 (Figure 21). This grille stands in the Puerta del Obispo Tenorio. Here the diagonals of one direction are square in section and those opposite are mere flat strips split to receive them, as explained by Figure 23. It is remarkable how much this simple scheme enhances the interest of the work. On a shield above the Tenorio grille is a charming bit of decorative iron relief apparently of the same period. Not unlike the Toledo example is a reja on the Pedro Dávila house in Avila (Figure 22). This reja and the window motif it is attached to are of the sixteenth century, much later than the rest of the palace.

Far more important than the lattice window grating is that made of typical Gothic bars conceived in the same spirit as the monumental church reja. Such window treatments frequently afford, along with the bossed doors, about the only adornment to the severe unpretentious façade of a Spanish palace. Their aspect, owing to the ornamental bar used, differs considerably from that of the Barcelona rejas with their plain round bars.

FIG. 23. DETAIL OF INTERSECTIONS. LATTICE WINDOW REJA.
House of Pedro Davila, Avila.   XVI Century.

FIG. 29. TOMB REJA OR VERJA.
Tomb of Bishop Diego de Anaya, Old Cathedral of Salamanca.
Circa 1450.

EASTON PUBLIC LIBRARY
EASTON PA

FIG. 30. REJA, CAPILLA DE SANTA ANA.
Burgos Cathedral. 1488

EASTON PUBLIC LIBRARY
EASTON PA

DEVELOPMENT OF THE VERTICAL BAR

Perhaps no single detail of Spanish ironwork underwent greater decorative expansion than the bar. As first encountered in the Romanesque reja of Pamplona (Figure 2) it is merely a flat vertical support for the scroll units which form the real body of the composition. Next, in the early Gothic examples from Barcelona the bar itself is the unit from which the whole work is built up. This bar is round, about one inch in diameter, and from twelve to fifteen feet high. Though severely plain, its making was a far more difficult task than the making of any ornamental motif in iron save the human figure. To work crude ingots into long attenuated and absolutely straight bars, round or square, was no mere apprentice's task; and indeed, considering that the appliances at the smith's disposal were very limited, the fashioning of such massive, well-finished, unwieldy rods must have been as expensive as it was difficult. A multiplicity of blows was necessary in the process, and the imprints of the smith's big square-headed hammer are still discernible (Figure 17). (Such a surface is particularly eloquent in contrast to that produced by modern over-perfected methods, and which smiths work over by hand in a vain attempt to catch some of the old charm.) When, later, the rectangular bar prevailed, its making was even more difficult for it added the new problem of keeping true angles. In both cases the smith acquitted himself well; then, having creditably mastered the severely plain form, he sought for some ornamental treatment that would enhance its interest without diminishing its strength. For this purpose the square vertical was better adapted than the round. It was first subjected while hot to a uniform torsion which, preserving the original arrises, resulted in a pleasing

FIG. 24. SPLIT BAR REJA.
Patio of the Count of Toledo's House, Toledo.

variation. Twisted throughout its entire length, it generally alternated with plain bars as in several Sigüenza examples (Figures 31 and 32); but just as often, it was twisted for only a short distance and then left untreated, which may also be seen at Sigüenza. For further enrichment, but this not until Renaissance days, the bar was sometimes incised with a

FIG. 32. CLOISTER REJA.
Cresting in color, Sigüenza Cathedral. 1508.

FIG. 31. CLOISTER REJA.
Cresting in color, Sigüenza Cathedral. 1508.

EASTON PUBLIC LIBRARY
EASTON PA

GOTHIC REJAS AND PULPITS 31

simple leaf pattern before being twisted, as in the Royal Chapel Reja of Granada (Figure 25); or its sides were beaten into a concavity in order to leave sharper arrises, as in the coro reja of Sevilla Cathedral (Figure 106); or, as in the same instance, a groove was cut in each side or a bead beaten up along its full length, all of which added great richness to the twist. Meanwhile the smith had discovered another variation that would lend patterning not merely to the bar itself but to the body of the reja as well. This was to split it at certain points and open it out into heart, lozenge, or trefoil outlines which he brought together again and welded back into a continuation of the

TOLEDO GRANADA SEVILLA

FIG. 26. TYPICAL PATTERNING INTO WHICH BARS WERE OPENED.

original rectangular rod (Figure 26). This idea of splitting the bars to create a band of patterning across the whole composition was carried to its ultimate point in the reja of the Royal Chapel at Granada (Figure 25). When nothing more could be devised to add interest to the rectangular bar, attention returned to the round, which was made into the Renaissance form known as the spindle, of which a fine specimen is in the Hispanic Society's collection, No. 165. For converting the spindle into a long, slender iron bar, Spain alone deserves the credit, since the only part it played in the Italian Renaissance was that of the stunted stone baluster which succeeded the carved or perforated parapet of Gothic balconies and staircases. The Spanish rejero on deciding to make the spindle out of iron used it timidly at first; but having soon surmounted the many difficulties it presented, as he had surmounted every other difficulty in ironwork, he began to turn out spindles by the thousands. The amazing skill attained in this new form will be discussed in the Renaissance chapter.

GOTICO-FLORIDO REJAS

The rejas to be taken up in the following pages belong to the Gotico-florido period, a very distinct and original phase in Spanish architecture. At a time when other nations were turning their attention to adopting the classic, Spain was accepting it but sparingly, and still clung to old Gothic traditions; thus in ironwork of the late fifteenth century Renaissance motifs were merely intermingled with earlier ones, but

FIG. 33. RUBBING OF UNDER PLATE OF
TRACERY BAND.

FIG. 34. RUBBING OF UPPER PLATE OF
TRACERY BAND.

FIG. 35. THE TWO PLATES RIVETED TOGETHER.
Middle XV Century.
Hispanic Society of America.
Length 16½ in., width 5½ in.   No. 147.

EASTON PUBLIC LIBRARY
EASTON PA

this in a way both picturesque and constructive; which cannot always be said of the stonework of the period, for here structurability was frequently lost sight of. Many Gotico-florido rejas, if judged away from their surroundings, might be pronounced too lavish; but in truth they are more reasonable than the florid, unstructural, carved stone framing them. Indeed, all through this transition in styles it is very evident that the ironworkers had a better hold on themselves than the architects, who, while being weaned away by the approaching Renaissance, merely toyed with the departing Gothic. The smith handled the transition better and was more alive to its opportunities. Whatever he caught from the approaching style, no matter how fanciful, he treated in sincerest Gothic manner and thus tied it in with the technique of the older work. Perhaps the most interesting survival of this period is that surrounding the Anaya tomb in Salamanca (Figure 29). Similar unrestraint in stonework would be weak; in iron it is a veritable *tour de force* and would be valuable if for no other reason than that it exhibits the unlimited possibilities of the metal.

Two of the most magnificent and best known Goticoflorido window rejas are also in Salamanca on the Casa de las Conchas, or House of the Shells, (Figures 27 and 28). The palace itself, however, is Renaissance and dates from 1512, offering one of many instances where the smith remained a Gothicist after the architect had accepted "the Italian taste." The two Casa Conchas designs are quite different from each other, for the old-time rejero never bound himself to conformity. One is rectangular, projects some fifteen inches from the wall, and is divided into three panels on its face. The twisted bar alternates with the plain, and all pass up behind the floriated arches and the lettered band. The castle of Castile is used to terminate the four main verticals, while the shell, indicating that the owner had made the holy pilgrimage to Santiago de Compostela, is used freely. Further indication of the owner's piety is found in the use of the "Ave Maria" in quaintly pierced iron letters, by way of an ornamental cross band. The other "Shell House" reja is the more striking of the two and is composed of three units, each a full semicircle in plan, and separated by several vertical bars. Both the tops and bottoms of these units are brought to an apex. With the exception of the inscription, the motifs of the ornament — turrets, shells and leaf tracery — are the same in both examples. In the patio of this same palace are other excellent grilles, but less magnificent than those of the façade.

A much plainer window reja, but of a sort whose popularity lasted even during the Renaissance, is shown in Figure 24. This faces on the patio of the Count of Toledo's home in Toledo, and is charmingly framed by glazed Moorish tiles. With such setting the ironwork needs but little ornamentation and this is supplied by the splitting of every other bar into an unusual sort of quatrefoil, and surmounting the whole by a band of leaf tracery and an armorial crest. In addition to being opened out into a pattern, the verticals are split to receive the horizontals instead of

FIG. 36. RUBBING OF UNDER PLATE OF
TRACERY BAND.

FIG. 37. RUBBING OF UPPER PLATE OF
TRACERY BAND.

FIG. 38. THE TWO PLATES RIVETED TOGETHER.
Middle XV Century.
Hispanic Society of America.
Length 16½ in., width 6 in.   No. 149.

EASTON PUBLIC LIBRARY
EASTON PA

vice versa. The method of putting together can be plainly seen in the illustration. The reja is built directly into the masonry, in somewhat the same manner as are basement grilles of to-day.

Among Gotico-florido tomb rejas or verjas are many of unsurpassed merit, one of the best known being in Salamanca's Romanesque or Old Cathedral (Figure 29), where it protects the effigy of Bishop Diego de Anaya, ambassador of Spain to the Council of Constance, who died in 1437. The screen is composed of square vertical bars twisted below and set on the diagonal above. At each corner are strongly accentuated posts whose panels are filled with richly modeled and perforated pointed foliage. Quite different in character are the central piers of the long side, being built up of numerous little buttresses with crocketed tops. Contrary to most screens of this period the verticals are much intercepted by horizontal bands of increasing richness above. The central band is made up of Gothic letters, as in the "Ave Maria" grille, spelling here the Archbishop's name. To give further interest, a twisted vine with innumerable tendrils — a very German motif — spreads from bar to bar. The crowning frieze is by far the richest thing of its day, a curious mingling of popular Gothic motifs and embryonic classic forms most unclassically wrought. In this cresting no trace of German or Flemish influence can be found; it is an entirely Spanish interpretation of classic. Candelabra, griffins and acanthus scroll make their appearance for the first time in any material since the remote days of the Roman occupation of Spain. Perhaps the smith worked as closely as he knew how from his classic models, whatever they may have been, but the result is pure Gothic in feeling and execution. No more exuberant mingling of pagan figures with Gothic could be found in any land. It is a truly remarkable bit of work viewed both from the historical and the artistic standpoint. The grille dates from about 1450.

At the monastery of Miraflores, a few miles out of Burgos, is the tomb of Don Juan II and his wife Isabella of Portugal. Enclosing it is an excellent Gothic low grille with split bars surmounted by a beautiful cresting of meandering Gothic forms and topped by diminutive crenellations, with colored heraldic shields in the freize to add to its splendor. Heraldic ornament, here mentioned for the first time, was destined to become one of the principal motifs in Renaissance ironwork. The Miraflores reja was made about 1480. Following its inspiration, a number of the tomb rails in Burgos cloisters introduce the family blazon with much prominence. Others executed about the same time may be seen at Zamora.

Of chapel rejas in the late Gothic style, the Santa Ana, in Burgos Cathedral (Figure 30) is highly important. The chapel itself was built between 1477 and 1488 and holds the tomb of its founder, Bishop de Acuña. As the architect was Simon of Cologne, one finds quite natural the several traces of German design in the reja. The lower part is a simple arrangement of bars divided into two stages by a charming band of flamboyant tracery; a similar band accentuated by the

FIG. 40. FLAMBOYANT GOTHIC PULPIT.
Avila Cathedral. Circa 1520.

FIG. 41. WROUGHT IRON HINGES.
Church of San Millán, Segovia.

projecting turrets of Castile crowns the bars and forms a base for the cresting. Thus far the grille is Spanish, but in the cresting the German tinge is apparent, particularly in the attenuated pinnacles built up of three separate rods. The intervening design is of beautiful foliation arranged in an unusual way. In the center, and quite Spanish again, is a superb blazon, the Acuña arms with a rampant griffin at each side. This motif is here much more emphasized than in the Miraflores verja.

Sigüenza Cathedral, a famous late Romanesque monument, holds an imposing display of rejas, some Gotico-florido and some Renaissance. The former are in the cloisters which, built much later than the cathedral, are in the late Gothic style, but with a few beautiful doorways in Plateresque (Renaissance). The rejas to the Plateresque portals exhibit less traces than the stonework of the coming style, as may be observed in Figures 31 and 32. Both rejas are made up of square bars set on the angle, twisting towards the top and opening out into various shapes, and in both examples the horizontal member has ceased to be strictly utilitarian, and has become an ornamented band. In each case the ornament is typical Italian detail but worked in a manner purely Gothic. Both crestings are also Plateresque but of a fifteenth century Gothic feeling, and are painted in colors. This is particularly effective in Figure 31, where the heraldic device is worked up in gold, red, and blue, while the supporting (and now headless) figures are gold and blue.

THE APPLICATION OF PAINT AND GILT TO IRON

With the use of armorial bearings as a decorative motif the painting and gilding of iron became natural and legitimate. Color demarcation was, in fact, an absolute necessity for the proper significance of the feature in question and the iron designer was only too happy to turn the necessity into a virtue. It is a proof of his good taste that he limited polychrome treatment to heraldry, instead of applying it to more extended areas. The surface of wrought iron has, as a result of much hammering, a peculiarly subtle interest; to cover or conceal this with a coating even as thin as liquefied oil paint would have robbed the material of its charm and given it the aspect of modern ironwork (wherein it is impossible, because of black paint, to discover the original quality of the work). In olden times the methods used for coloring iron were much the same as to-day, but with a difference in the ingredients. It was first necessary to apply a "fixing" coat to the metal which would act as an adhesive for the oil paint. For this purpose a much diluted glue was generally used which, in addition to serving as a fixative, was so transparent as not to effect the final coloring. That there was no special art required to paint iron may be assumed from the fact it was commonly executed by the image painter, *pintor de imaginería* — the man employed by the church for coloring retablos, images, picture frames, and sacred furnishings in general. What has been said about coloring is in a measure true of gilding ironwork, namely: that no finish is com-

FIG. 42. CRUDE DOOR KNOCKER.
Probably early XVI Century.
Hispanic Society of America.
Height of backplate 8½ in.   No. 48.

parable to that left by the hammer of the smith. Nevertheless the gold leaf, because of its method of application, is more sympathetic than brushed-on color. At the period when gilding certain portions, even entire rejas, came into favor in Spain — that is, at the height of the Renaissance — gold was streaming in from the recent conquests in America. Little ingots were beaten into leaves of an almost infinitesimal thinness, which were dipped in poppy oil and then beaten to the iron. It will be seen that by this process much of the original interest of the iron surface was still discernible after the gilding. Another but less frequent method of applying gold was to beat it to a powder in a mortar and pestel, then mix it with either poppy oil or glue and paint it on with a brush. Chemically prepared gilt and bronze powders, such as are generally used to-day, were unknown to the Spanish worker; fortunately, too, for their use would have passed out of the artist's hands and become, as now, a mere journeyman-painter's task. Sevilla Cathedral contains the finest examples of rejas completely gilded. Good examples of painted motifs making rich spots in a large composition may be encountered in scores of churches, none, however, more magnificent than the blazon of Charles V in the Royal Chapel reja of Granada (Figure 108).

THE HORIZONTAL MEMBER

Difficulty of removal has made it almost impossible for collectors to possess a large reja *in toto*, but numerous fragments such as bars, spindles, cross bands, and even entire crestings have been secured; of these a cresting and a number of bands or borders, in which different kinds of execution may be studied, are owned by the Hispanic Society. The ornamental horizontal is, as previously stated, the evolution of the simple structural flat member of early days. At first it was threaded at regular intervals to receive the uprights; when it became a modest ornamental feature, the uprights passed behind it as in the Casa Conchas examples; and finally, when it expanded into the broad and marvelously rich piece of work seen in Renaissance rejas, it altogether interrupted the verticals into short lengths. This meant that the structural part formerly played by each individual upright was now confined to a certain few full-length pilasters and piers, which were stoutly proportioned to meet the demands made on them (Figure 25). Of the elaboration of the band by means of lettering pierced *à jour* the Ave Maria (Figure 27) furnishes an excellent example. Leaf and geometric patterns pierced through a single sheet of iron in early days and later through several superimposed sheets, offered another means of securing ornamental effect (Figures 33 to 38). The earliest pieces in this style were cut with absolutely flat, untreated edges, as in the lock plate on Figure 15; but later when several layers of metal were used the pattern edge was sometimes carefully beveled. As Gothic passed into Gotico-florido, these simple flat treatments were felt to be inadequate for the richness and movement of the composition, and modeling in high relief was practiced. It was obtained by repoussé work — the

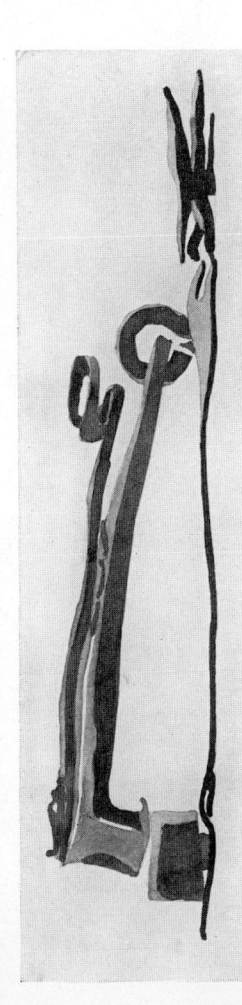

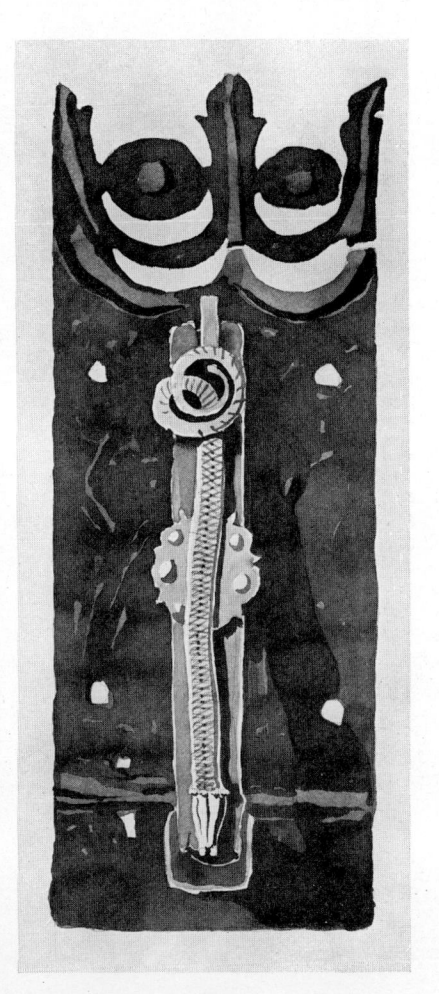

FIG. 43. DOOR KNOCKER.
Showing early use of crown motif. Late XIV Century.
Hispanic Society of America.
Height 10 in., width 4 in.   No. 47.

GOTHIC REJAS AND PULPITS

beating out of the pattern by blows from the back —
and may be encountered either alone or, as in Figure
39, in combination with piercing. Among the various
bands illustrated, the flamboyant tracery pieces (Figures 35 and 38) are particularly interesting to the
student since it has been possible to obtain rubbings
of their separate parts. Figure 33 is the foundation
plate of Figure 35, rubbed from the back, and it appears
much denser and less transparent than in the finished
work, after the very open upper plate (Figure 34) has
been applied to it. Both sheets are about one-sixteenth
of an inch thick, and are fitted together with such nicety
that it is almost impossible to determine, until after
close examination, whether the work is not done from
one thickness of metal cut in two planes. These same
observations apply to Figure 38 and its separate rubbings where the pattern is even more intricate and
refined.

As a stiffener for the band and a better means for
applying it to the reja, a strip of iron usually runs
along both top and bottom, back and front, and is
riveted to the pattern. Such strips generally take the
form of a moulding, the execution of which is strangely

FIG. 39. FOLIATED BAND.
Pierced and Beaten in Repoussé. Late XV Century.
Hispanic Society of America.
Length 2 ft. 2 in., width 6 in.   No. 153.

crude even where the band is most refined. This disparity is to be explained by the fact that it was a much more difficult task to beat out a good architectural moulding of even the simplest section than to execute piercing or repoussé work. Bands similar to those described, but smaller, were made in great quantity for chests; and being easily portable are eagerly sought by collectors.

GOTHIC PULPITS

Besides the reja another peculiarly Spanish production was the iron pulpit, often designed in conjunction with it. This, like the Gothic reja, is not as frequent as in the succeeding period, but a few examples of fine design and workmanship may be found at Avila and Burgos, among other places. Pulpits are generally in pairs, one at each side of the Capilla Mayor, and are used for the reading of the gospel and epistle respectively. A single one, a drawing of which may be found in Street's Gothic Architecture on Spain, stands in the small church of San Gil at Burgos. There is very little about this work that has to do with real smithery, the faces of its hexagonal form being divided into vertical panels of delicate Gothic patterning which are produced by superimposed pierced plates riveted to a wooden frame. The pulpit is supported on a standard rather *pauvre* and ungraceful, and is attached besides to one of the nave piers. It dates from the end of the fifteenth century.

The Avila example (Figure 40) is far more beautiful and interesting both as a piece of architectural design

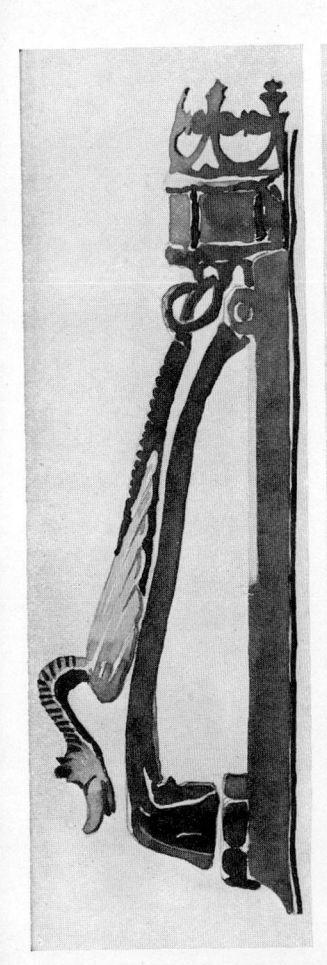

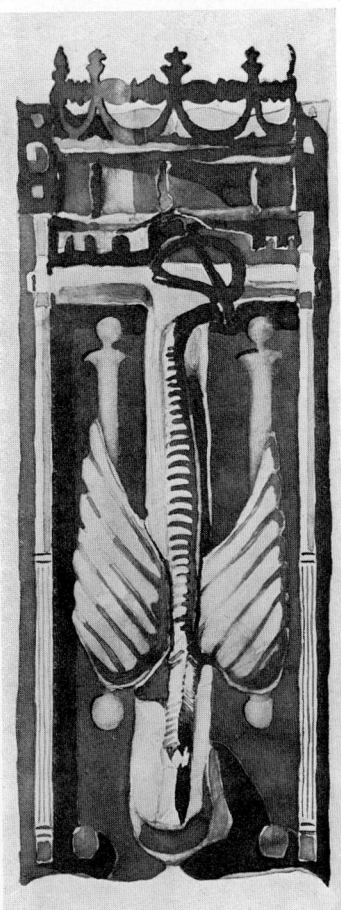

FIG. 44. GOTHIC-RENAISSANCE DOOR KNOCKER.
Early XVI Century.
Hispanic Society of America.
Height 11 in., width 4¼ in.   No. 49.

and as ironwork. It is flamboyant Gothic, although erected at the same time as its Renaissance companion and probably by the same master — supposed to be the rejero Juan Francés who executed the rejas for the capilla mayor and for the coro of the cathedral. Both pulpits are of gilded iron, hexagonal in plan, ten feet in height, and the body of each bears the arms of the cathedral, namely, the *Agnus Dei*, the lion, and the castle, all surmounted by a crown. Here the similarity ends, for the body of the pulpit in question is in pure flamboyant Gothic of strongly Flemish flavor. The accessories, however — the standard, brackets, staircase, and rail — are Renaissance; yet the ensemble, due to a most intelligent observance of scale, is perfectly congruous. The sides of the pulpit, including that which opens as a gate, are divided into upper and lower halves by an ornamental band, and these are divided vertically by a delicate crocketed pinnacle. The tracery is about the same in all the twenty-four panels, except for those little discrepancies which make up the charm of Gothic ironwork. One marvels at the author who dared to pick out such a specially difficult phase of geometric tracery requiring, as it did, the greatest nicety of calculation and execution. The delicate modeling of this tracery into planes is obtained by the familiar method of riveting together successive sheets cut to form the pattern. It is not an attempt to copy a carved wooden pulpit in iron, for everywhere the rivet heads have been accentuated rather than concealed; by following their outline the size of each sheet of metal is clearly determined.

These rivets go through to the oak frame on which the work is built up. 1520 is generally accepted as the date of this production.

Far later than this, but likewise embodying both Gotico-florido and Renaissance forms, is the iron pulpit from the church of San Salvador in Cortejana in the province of Estremadura. In this case there is no wooded framework, the whole being built up of solid bar iron richly wrought in florid forms. It is of German aspect, but was wrought long after Spain's intercourse with the Low Countries had ceased —as late, in fact, as the seventeenth century. Other examples, good, but not strikingly fine, may be seen at either side of the capilla mayor in Murcia Cathedral. Many more pulpits than are here mentioned were undoubtedly made but were done away with, or in some cases replaced by Renaissance, when the old Gothic position and arrangement of the coro was changed. This change, which will be described later, came in Renaissance times, and probably caused the discarding of much fine Gothic work.

FIG. 45. GOTHIC–RENAISSANCE DOOR KNOCKER.
Early XVI Century.
Hispanic Society of America.
Height 10¾ in., width 4 in.   No. 50.

EASTON PUBLIC LIBRARY
EASTON PA

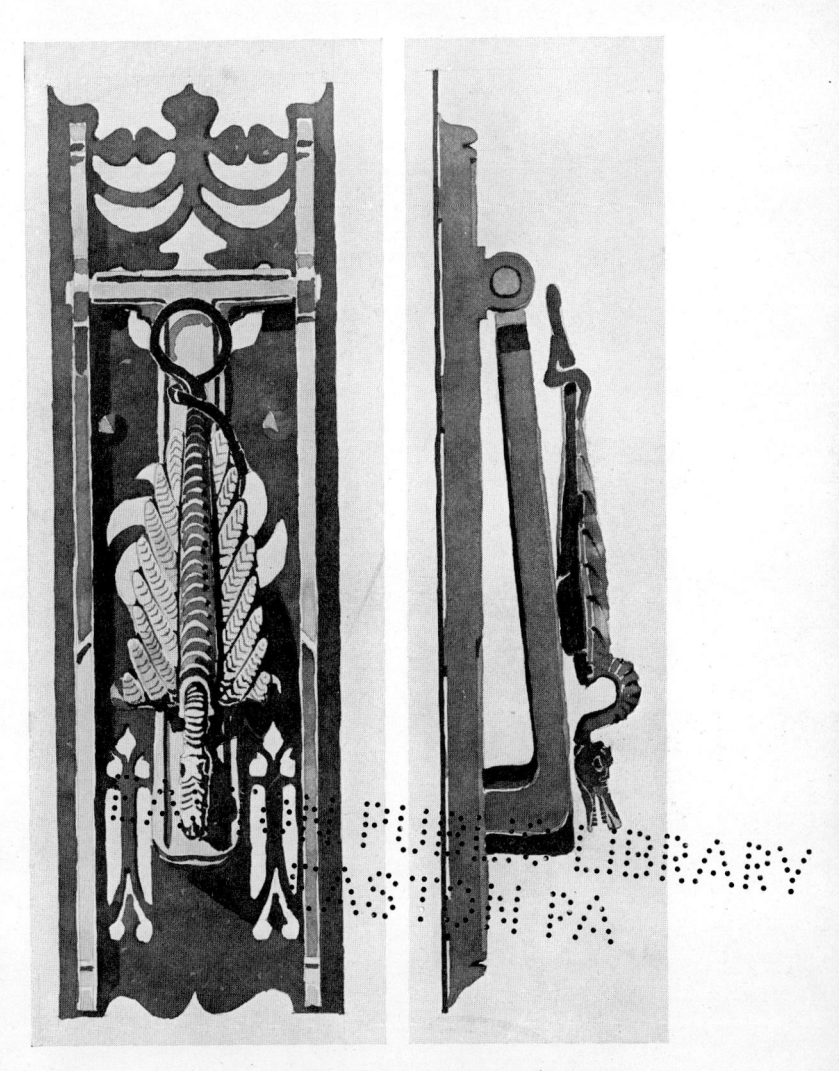

FIG. 46. GOTHIC–RENAISSANCE DOOR KNOCKER.
About 1600.
Hispanic Society of America.
Height 12½ in., width 4¼ in.   No. 51.

EASTON PUBLIC LIBRARY
EASTON PA

III
GOTHIC HARDWARE AND DOMESTIC UTENSILS

KNOCKERS

AS Gothic architecture matured in France and Western Europe in general, it demanded a richly carved and paneled wooden door which left no space for the spreading iron hinges so popular in the beginning of the style; but in Spanish Gothic this typical carved door never succeeded in supplanting the flat Moorish one sheathed in metal or studded with nailheads. Even in Toledo Cathedral, where certain Gothic structural features (the vaulting of the ambulatory, for instance) are carried further than in any French prototype, the massive main doors and several interior ones are Moorish in type.

The Moorish door is built up of an elaborate intersecting wooden frame which remains visible on the inside as a series of varying coffers, and is covered on the exterior with stout vertical boarding. Contrary to the carved Gothic door, which was so given over to a display of the wood-carver's skill that it left no room for metal decoration, this one presented its entire exterior for iron embellishment; in other words, there was a distinct difference between door hardware in Spain and in France or England; and this even from Romanesque and early Gothic times when the hinge was developed north of the Pyrenees to its uttermost decorative possibility, but in Spain was rarely featured. When, occasionally, an ornamental strap hinge was made, it closely resembled French prototypes as on the door of San Millan at Segovia (Figure 41). Generally it was kept within strictly utilitarian bounds and was fastened on the interior of the door. Exterior hinges and carved panels being conspicuously few, it is rather to the nailhead or bosse, the knocker, and the backplate, that one must look for the decorative finish of the flat Spanish door.

Next to the nailhead, whose making has already been described, the most characteristic bit of Spanish door hardware is the knocker (called *llamador* by the Spaniards and *aldabón* by the Moors). The first knockers were very simple, consisting of a flat backplate to which was riveted either a ring or a vertical hammer, the latter often dropping against a large plain nailhead. The backplate grew in time to be very elaborate, but at first it was unornamented and crude in outline. Even the crudest, however, contained the germ of an idea peculiarly Spanish and which was later very highly developed — the hood over the vertical knocker (Figure 42). It was with the solid hammer of the first knockers that the smith was most concerned. For this he went to nature for his inspiration and fashioned archaic men, birds, lizards, etc., extremely quaint, but devoid of the architecturalizing that later appeared in even the smallest accessories. From these beginnings down to the end the development of the knocker may be studied

FIG. 50. DOOR KNOCKER WITH
DOUBLE BOSSE.
Late XVI Century.
Hispanic Society of America.
Total Height 14 in.   No. 70.

FIG. 49. DOOR KNOCKER WITH A
SINGLE BOSSE.
Late XVI Century.
Hispanic Society of America.
Total height 10½ in.   No. 104.

EASTON PUBLIC LIBRARY
EASTON PA

GOTHIC HARDWARE AND UTENSILS 47

in the Hispanic Society's collection, from which most of the following illustrations of door hardware are taken.

Almost primitive in appearance are Figures 42 and 43, produced north of the Ebro. These are early Gothic in period but Romanesque in spirit, although their dirth of ornamentation makes it difficult to place them with any degree of certainty. They may even have been made as late as the beginning of the fifteenth century in some remote district of Catalonia, Navarre, or Aragón, which had never been penetrated by either pure Gothic or Saracenic. It is their frankly crude workmanship rather than any merit of design that makes them interesting. Over the backplate in Figure 42, as already mentioned, may be seen the crude hood or canopy which will be recognized later in the rich crowns, semi-circular in form, which remained a feature of Spanish knockers even through Renaissance days. In Figure 43 it is the ornament at the top of the backplate which, when much refined, became the typical adornment of the crown motif just described. The lack of stability and finish at the sides of this backplate seems to have disturbed the smith, for we find him in Figure 44 adding attenuated buttresses invisibly riveted from the back; and in Figure 45 still further architecturalizing his work by cabled edging surmounted by diminutive pinnacles. Buttresses were treated in many ways and in addition to cabling were sometimes splayed and chamfered. In Figures 44 and 45 both backplates are cut from metal one-sixteenth of an inch thick and

48 GOTHIC HARDWARE AND UTENSILS

pierced in the manner which had now become popular and which in this instance is of Renaissance outline at the top. The lizard adorning the hammer (Figure 44) was widely used in France as well as Spain during this period; the extent to which it was refined may be seen in Figure 46 and Figure 70. The same features were generally followed: — outstretched wings beautifully etched and engraved, arched neck of scales, and ringed tail; but in Figure 46 the work is

FIG. 47. ARCHAIC HAMMER OF A XV CENTURY DOOR KNOCKER.

Hispanic Society of America. Height 12 in. No. 54.

FIG. 48. ARCHAIC HAMMER OF A XV CENTURY DOOR KNOCKER.

Hispanic Society of America. Height 7 in. No. 53.

FIG. 52. PILGRIM SHELL KNOCKER.
Early XVII Century.
Hispanic Society of America. No. 75.
Total height 9½ in.

FIG. 51. STIRRUP KNOCKER.
XVII Century.
Hispanic Society of America. No. 103.
Total height 10½ in.

EASTON PUBLIC LIBRARY
EASTON PA

GOTHIC HARDWARE AND UTENSILS 49

so mathematically precise and so accurately cut that much of the charm of the earlier examples is lost.

Probably contemporaneous with Figures 42 and 43 are Figures 47 and 48, also curiously archaic, but likewise not as old as would appear at first glance, and with the metal hammered into a much greater density than in previous examples. Both may be fifteenth century work. The immemorial *boina* or Basque cap of the man places one of these pieces at least as coming from the northern provinces; an impression further borne out by the purplish tinge of the iron, Biscayan ore being remarkable for its rich purple color. Probably neither of these figures was ever furnished with a backplate, a nailhead placed under the hammer sufficing for the necessary resonance. Of the two, the tailless dog, whose feet rest on a little cushion after the conventional manner of the dog on Gothic tombs, is less primitive looking. Another early fifteenth century piece is No. 52 in the Hispanic collection, a curious little dragon with a shield on his back. The heavy bar which forms the frame of this knocker and to which the beast is fastened, is hinged onto two projecting stanchions. This is a fine bit of smithing with good back riveting.

Bosses, singly or in pairs with one placed above the other, were found to serve very well as supports for the knocker (Figure 49), thus doing away with the backplate; but the bosse, although a Moorish feature, was often treated in a way which might be classed as Gothic. In Figure 50 it is beaten out into naturalistic leaf forms, and in Figure 52 the two separate units are made of rosettes, each concentric layer cut

50   GOTHIC HARDWARE AND UTENSILS

to a different pattern so as to give a flower-like effect — a motif often found in later Renaissance objects. This knocker introduces the pilgrims' shell, a favorite motif in Castile. Going back to Figures 50 and 51, we find the hammer bent from a rectangular bar and suggesting the patterns into which reja verticals were often opened out for decorative effect.

Figure 53, one of a massive pair, is a splendid example of Gothic smithing. The hammer is of the popular flattened ring type found all over Spain, and its ends, instead of being welded together, may be seen terminating separately where they pass through

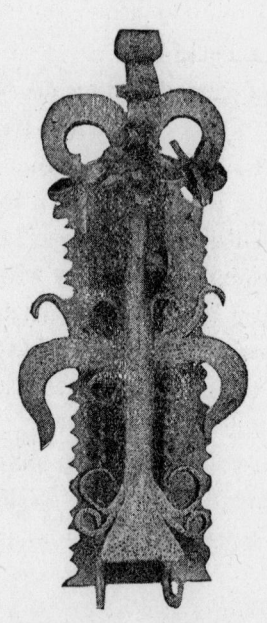

FIG. 55.   KNOCKER.
Gothic in spirit but probably XVIII Century work.
Hispanic Society of America.
Height 18 in.   No. 117.

FIG. 53. ONE OF A PAIR OF GOTHIC DOOR
KNOCKERS.
XV Century.   Hispanic Society of America.
Total height 13 in.   Nos. 71 and 73.
FIG. 54. DOOR KNOCKER OF MUDÉJAR DESIGN.
XVII Century.   Hispanic Society of America.
Total Height 13 in.   No. 86.

GOTHIC HARDWARE AND UTENSILS

the beast's head. The contour of the ring is pleasingly irregular and the modeling, owing to the inconspicuousness of the punch marks, is felt all over the surface. The horned head, especially around the open mouth, is beautifully wrought and shows no sign of supplementary tooling. Such a piece might well have been a warning to later smiths who so ornamented their surface as to conceal its forging. Another good piece of smithing, but one which may not be over a hundred and fifty years old, is Figure 55. While entirely forged, it assembles many of the motifs used by those who worked the metal while cold — the chief reason for suspecting it to be more modern than its forging appears. Whatever its date, it is interesting as exhibiting the limit to which smithery on a small scale could be carried.

Old hardware is often difficult to place as to period owing to its original door having rotted away and the piece under consideration having been applied to the newer door. Then, too, artistic movements even as great and widespread as the Renaissance traveled slowly in Spain. Important towns like Avila and Segovia, for instance, never really shook off medievalism, and their artisans went on producing Gothic long after others were working in the "Italian taste." For this reason it is necessary to have a knowledge of local art and history to determine the age of an object and whether its style is indigenous or transplanted. This is very apparent in examining the iron in the Vich Museum; for it contains pieces collected in outlying Pyrenean towns and authentically placed in the seventeenth century but which look as primitive as fourteenth century pieces produced in Barcelona.

THE EASTERN INFLUENCE IN KNOCKERS

Door ironwork passed in time from the simple smithing process into a combination of smithing with Eastern methods of enrichment applied when the metal was cold. As such treatment affected surface rather than form, the flat backplate was naturally the first part to undergo change. This was accomplished by notching and lobing it around the margin and piercing its center with Oriental and Gothic tracery or incising it with patterning. Figure 56 is one of the earliest departures; but here the forged bird is incised as well, its feathers being indicated by etching. In this same class is Number 56 in the Hispanic Society's collection, with a notched backplate and a curious S-shaped forged hammer in the form of a two-headed dragon whose scales have been elaborately chiseled.

In contrast to the above knockers, which in spite of Moorish treatment follow Gothic forms, are those of truly Oriental form with backplate invariably circular or star-shaped; these usually had a ring for a hammer and a separate bolt for a striker. The ring was also combined with an extremely small backplate — little more, in fact, than an anchorage for it (Figures 57 and 58). The circular backplate was pierced with Eastern patterns and its edge notched and serrated or perhaps finished with a cabled border. Of this class are Figures 59, 60, 61 and 62. Their

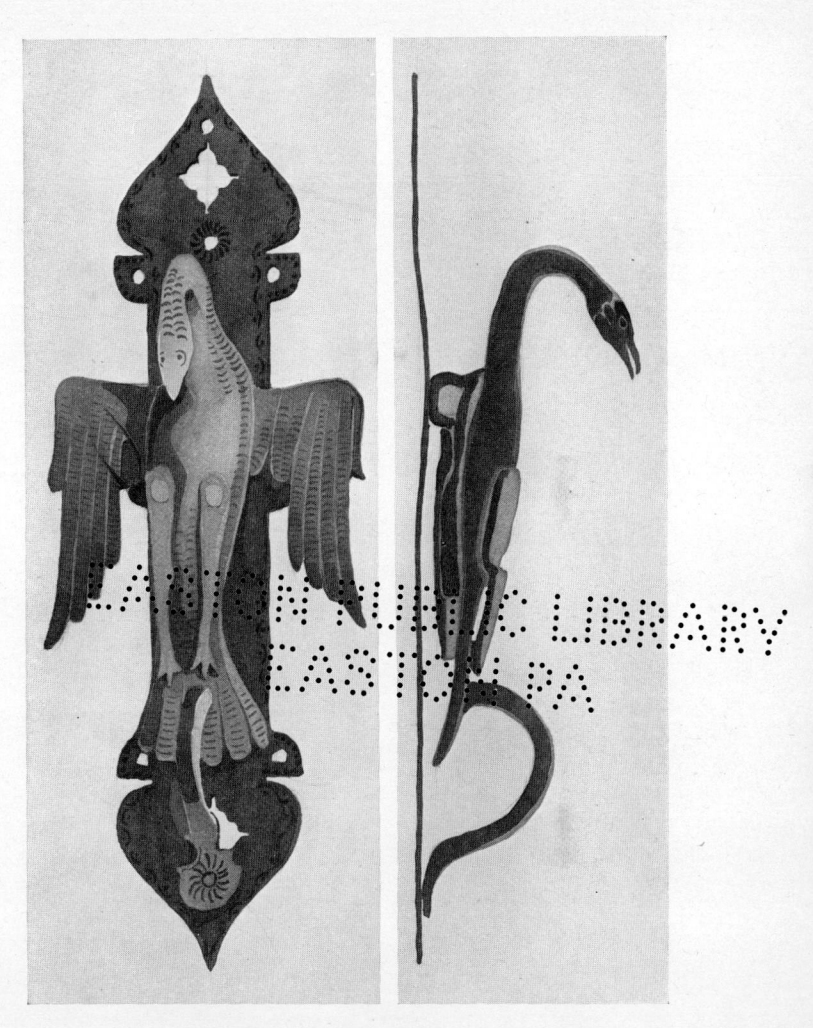

FIG. 56. DOOR KNOCKER WITH INCISED
PATTERNING.
Hispanic Society of America.
Height 13½ in.   No. 55.

EASTON PUBLIC LIBRARY
EASTON PA

FIG. 57. RING HANDLE
WITH CLINCH.
XVI Century.
Hispanic Society of America.
Dia. of ring 8 in. No. 61.

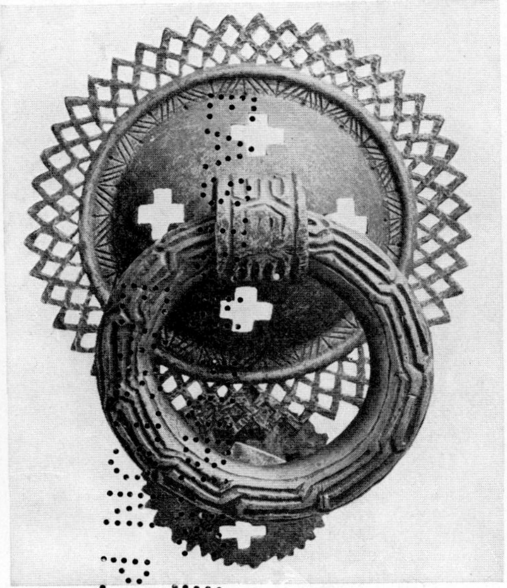

FIG. 59. RING KNOCKER OF
MOORISH INSPIRATION.
XVI Century.
Hispanic Society of America.
Dia. of ring 5 in. No. 91.

FIG. 58. RING HANDLE
WITH BOSSE.
XVI Century.
Hispanic Society of America.
Dia. of ring 5 in. No. 66.

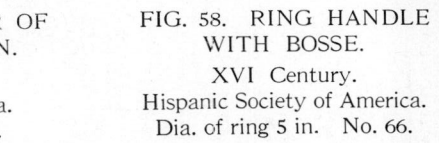

EASTON PUBLIC LIBRARY
EASTON PA

GOTHIC HARDWARE AND UTENSILS 53

rings do not depend solely on the smith's hammer for interest, but are treated with untiring patience by being pounced, lined and patterned. Even more Eastern as a conception is the star-shaped plate seen in Figure 63. This, as well as Figure 64, is a good Mudéjar example with Moorish and Gothic details successfully harmonized. In both the filagree of the backplate is interesting, for it shows how the scale of Gothic ornamentation can be reduced to a delicacy which is purely Oriental in appearance. It is not unlikely that these two pieces were made by Moorish

FIG. 65. DOOR KNOCKER WITH GOTHIC BACKPLATE.
XVII Century.
Hispanic Society of America.
Height 9½ in. No. 110.

artizans working long after Christian rule had been established.

Gothic considerably architecturalized is seen in Figure 65, which immediately precedes the flamboyant seen in Figures 66 and 67. In this Gotico-florido period when stone itself, in spite of its limitations, was as intricately cut as if it were soft wood, it is not surprising to find the ironworker likewise overstepping the limits of his stubborn material, and reaching a laciness hardly surpassed by gold and silver workers. The basis of his knocker design was the rich flamboyant stonework of the day, and the figure used as a striker was not forged, but chiseled out of the solid iron. Backplates too were extremely rich, often chiseled and beveled as well as pierced, as if labor counted for nothing; and in proportion as excessive labor was expended on an object the theory of good structure was neglected. The lacelike openness of the backplate in Figure 67 represents a prodigious amount of patient cutting in each of the two pierced sheets, and these are so ingeniously riveted together as to appear like one thickness of metal beveled. While in a general way this piece resembles a typical French flamboyant knocker, it has a Spanish appearance because of the Eastern patterning incised up the sides of the buttresses and on the neck of the winged beast; the tracery crowning each panel is likewise very Spanish, as seen in the semicircular crown motif already mentioned. How much further this ornateness might have been carried if Renaissance had not made its appearance is problematical.

FIG. 60. RING HANDLE OF ORIENTAL DESIGN.
Late XVI Century.
Hispanic Society of America.
Dia. of ring 5½ in. No. 89.

FIG. 61. DOOR KNOCKER OF ORIENTAL INSPIRATION.
About 1600.
Hispanic Society of America.
Dia. of ring 6 in. No. 99.

FIG. 62. DOOR KNOCKER OF ORIENTAL DESIGN.
Late XVI Century.
Hispanic Society of America.
Dia. of ring 4½ in. No. 97.

GOTHIC HARDWARE AND UTENSILS

Indicating the flamboyant artizan's attempt to grasp the Renaissance are Figures 68 and 69 which, for the sake of sequence, may be termed *transitional*. In both cases the backplate has lost its Gothic buttresses and pinnacles and instead is enclosed in a severe moulded frame — a Renaissance idea. As might be expected, the mitering is inaccurate; the predecessors of this struggling Renaissance craftsman would not have tolerated such a method of making a frame but would have bent the entire moulding from a straight bar. Rich flamboyant tracery has here been

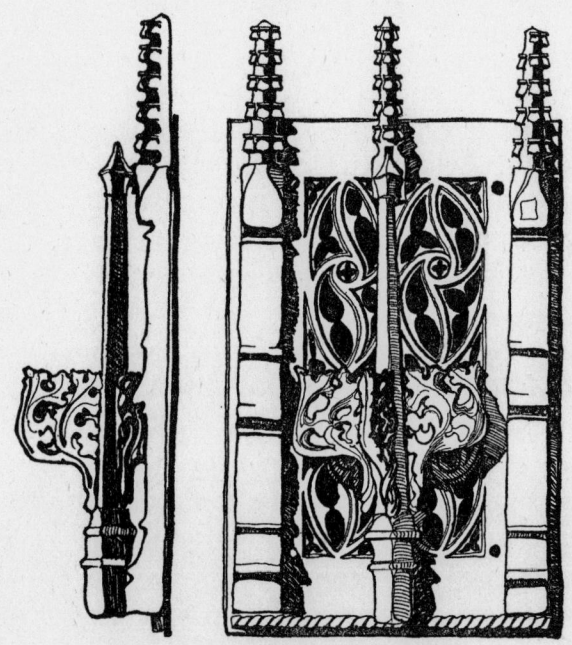

FIG. 66. GOTHIC KNOCKER.
Late XVI Century.
Hispanic Society of America.
Height of backplate 6½ in. No. 106.

abandoned for a simple leaf pattern neither Gothic nor Renaissance; the two forged hammers are likewise much simplified. This particular ornamentation is very Aragonese in character, and it is probable that these two pieces were made in that province long after the Gothic had passed away elsewhere. In this same class, but exhibiting slightly more of Renaissance understanding, are Figures 70, 71, and 72; the last with the round-headed classic arch crudely cut through the backplate.

LOCKS AND HASPS

Spanish locks, while artistic, never received the same amount of attention from the ironworker as did knockers, except in the case of those made for the vargueño, a characteristic piece of Spanish furniture which will be mentioned later. Lock-making for doors never became the fine art it was in France, where the French smith, assimilating the methods and skill of the locksmith, armorer, and jeweler, produced locks so exquisitely wrought that they have since found a place in all considerable collections of art works. There are nevertheless some excellent Spanish locks in the Hispanic collection; but the majority, as indicated by their hinged hasps, were originally affixed to trunks and chests. In the illustrations of Romanesque and early Gothic rejas can be seen the simple locks of those periods; the device being the slide bolt with attached hasp which, when released, served as a handle as well. Such a lock, or rather bolt, was necessarily large and crude, for anything of small

FIG. 64. DOOR HANDLE WITH
MUDÉJAR TRACERY.
Late XVI Century.
Hispanic Society of America.
Dia. of backplate 9 in.   No. 95.

FIG. 63. DOOR KNOCKER WITH
MUDÉJAR TRACERY.
LATE XVI Century.
Hispanic Society of America.
Dia. of backplate 10¼ in.   No. 96.

EASTON PUBLIC LIBRARY
EASTON PA

GOTHIC HARDWARE AND UTENSILS

scale and greater nicety would have failed to adjust itself to the structural discrepancies in these big, heavy gates; but even Renaissance rejeros appreciated its suitability for the reja and continued using it, considerably enriched, throughout the sixteenth century (Figure 103).

Common to all Europe was the lock which, dispensing with the bolt, consisted of hasp, lockplate and box, the whole being fastened in position by means of fixing staples. Of these last, an early specimen, rather crude, holds the knocker of Figure 45 in place. The fixing staple having proven itself to be the strongest means of fastening down the lockplate, it was used in varying form throughout all periods and became in the Spanish Renaissance a work of art in itself that sometimes overshadowed the rest of the lock. Typical Gothic ones are seen in the fifteenth century lock in Figure 73. This is of crude flamboyant workmanship and the traceried band was once gilded. It and Figure 74 are typical of the period — square or oblong panels of tracery treated architecturally, a decorated hasp often in the form of an archaic figure, and some moveable feature to conceal the keyhole; this last, as seen in Figure 74, sometimes took the form of a Biblical personage under a canopy. A rather amusing innovation in this piece is the four corner heads used instead of staples to hold the lock fast.

A rich late Gothic lock and hasp, and one with a more distinctively Spanish treatment than the two last mentioned, is Figure 76. Pieces almost identical

58 GOTHIC HARDWARE AND UTENSILS

to it existed in the splendid collection of the Duque de Segovia, which was recently sold outside of Spain. Figure 76 consists of an ornamental backplate with a very much raised lockbox, the former held down at the corners by four beautifully worked rosettes,

FIG. 75. CHEST LOCK WITH FALSE FIXING STAPLES OVER KEYHOLE.
Late XVI Century.
Hispanic Society of America.
Backplate 6 in. square. No. 108.

between which the plate is perforated with fish tracery forming a border around the lockbox; in addition to this treatment, the edges are scalloped and the remaining surface engraved in the Moorish fashion. The hasp (which is out of position in the illustration)

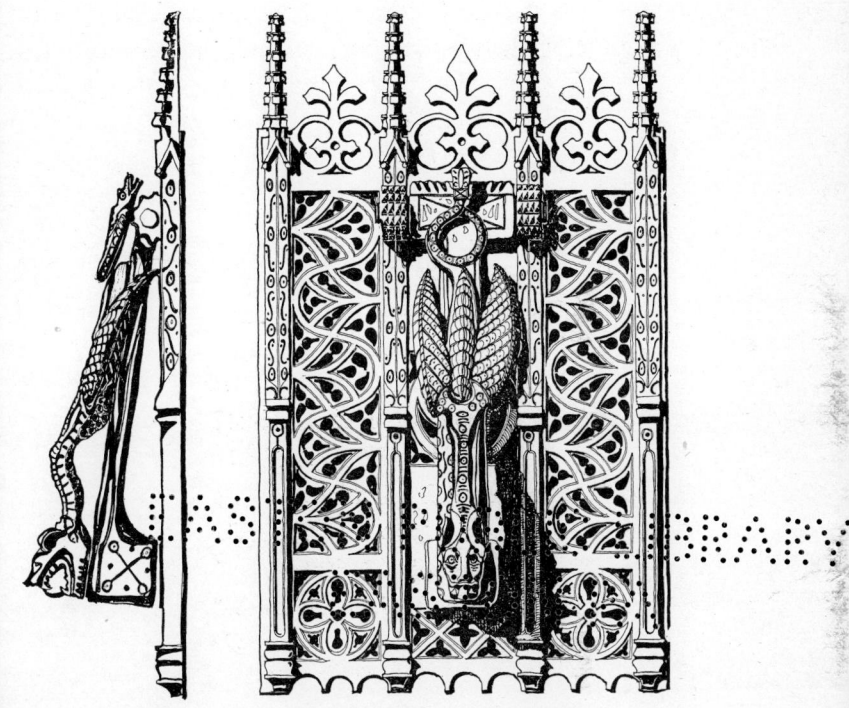

FIG. 67. RICH FLAMBOYANT KNOCKER.
Middle XVI Century.
Hispanic Society of America.
Height 10 in., width 6 in.   No. 111.

GOTHIC HARDWARE AND UTENSILS 59

is treated with as much attention as the backplate. Its lower part, raised to fit over the lockbox, is perforated and engraved, and on it lies a little lizard-like beast with curled tongue and tail. At the top this hasp widens out to fourteen inches and is much engraved with the vine pattern, strongly suggesting the form and patterning of German work; this por-

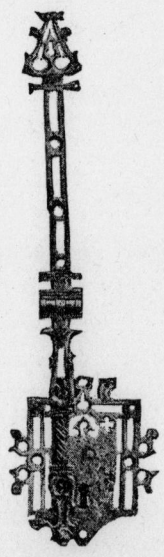

FIG. 80. LOCKPLATE AND HASP.
Probably XVII Century.
Hispanic Society of America.
Length 14 in.   No. 115.

tion is skillfully welded to the bar at the top. There is no indication of how this huge hasp was fastened or hinged to its object;—probably by staples which passed over the end of the bar, but are now missing.

Hasps as well as fixing staples received great

attention from the locksmith. As the nature of the hasp did not allow much latitude of form, the long narrow strip used at the beginning endured throughout all periods, but the manner of decorating it changed with each epoch. Owing to its being attached separately from the lock, and being, besides, the more fragile member, the hasp is frequently missing in old locks. Figures 76 to 79 are good examples of late Gothic running into Renaissance.

CHEST AND BOX FITTINGS

Throughout the ages caskets and chests have always received great attention from the artizan. As iron came into its own in the Middle Ages, we find chests and strong boxes in that metal produced in all the countries of Europe; but far more numerous, because less ponderous, were wooden boxes with iron trimmings. Such objects answered the manifold uses of the yet unborn wardrobe or chest of drawers. The humblest as well as the noblest dwellings were supplied with them, so that the chest-maker, especially in the thirteenth and fourteenth centuries, was one of the busiest artizans in any land. The large sized chest, called in Spain an *arcón*, served also as a seat and, when covered with a straw mattress, as a bed; and was so solidly constructed and reinforced with iron strips as to be practically indestructible. Of early Spanish chests one of the best known is that said to have belonged to the Cid and now in Burgos Cathedral, with many iron rings indicating that it was a baggage chest to be fastened to the back of a sumpter

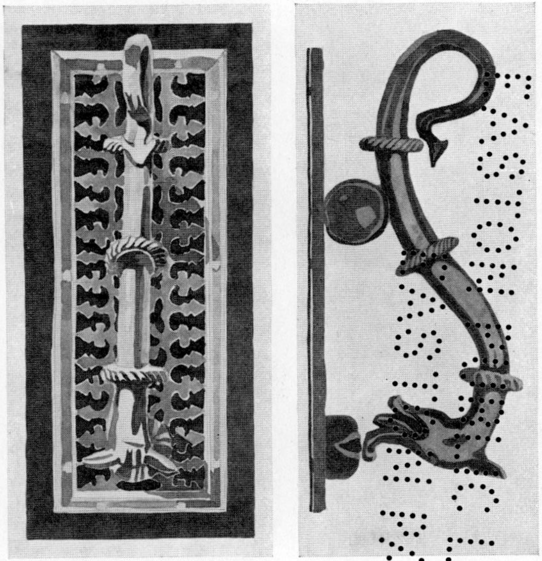

FIG. 68. KNOCKER OF ARAGONESE TYPE.
XVII Century.
Hispanic Society of America.
Height 10½ in., width 4 in.　　No. 125.

FIG. 69. KNOCKER OF ARAGONESE TYPE.
XVII Century.
Hispanic Society of America.
Height 10¼ in., width 4¼ in.　　No. 123.

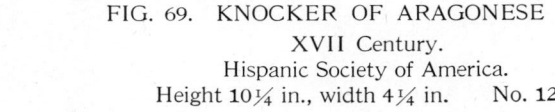

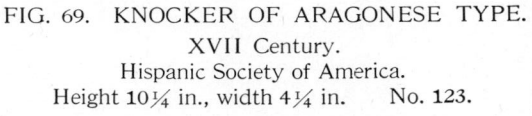

EASTON PUBLIC LIBRARY
EASTON PA

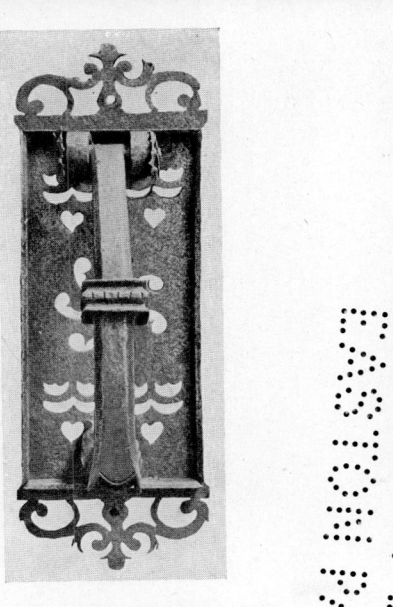

FIG. 70. DOOR KNOCKER.
Tentative Renaissance but made
in the XVII Century.
Hispanic Society of America.
Total height 13 in. No. 138.

FIG. 71. DOOR KNOCKER
WITH OPEN BACKPLATE.
XVII Century.
Hispanic Society of America.
Total height 12 in. No. 142.

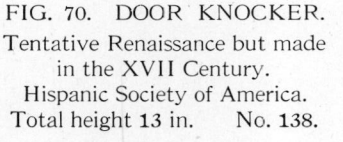

FIG. 72. DOOR KNOCKER OF
EARLY RENAISSANCE
DESIGN.
About 1600.
Hispanic Society of America.
Total height 14 in. No. 122.

EASTON PUBLIC LIBRARY
EASTON PA

GOTHIC HARDWARE AND UTENSILS

mule. Spanish chests of a small, portable size were frequently covered with hide or parchment which was painted red; or sometimes the covering was left its natural color and the iron straps painted vermillion. Later, in addition to these necessary iron straps and clamps, were added iron rosettes, plaques, numerous hinges and double locks, all beautifully wrought. The smallest chests, for guarding jewels, missals, and other little objects, were called *arquetas* and were sometimes made entirely of iron as elaborately chiseled as was the small ivory box of the Moors. In the fifteenth century the jewel box was provided with little drawers and was thence known as a *huche*.

One type of small casket is that which figured in the inventory of Margaret of Spain in 1524 as "bien ouvré à jour" in the "manière d'Espagne." It consisted of a somewhat flat rectangular box with slightly ridged lid and was covered with parallel rows of repeating tracery patterns worked out of two thicknesses of pierced plate and half round wire. Such boxes were usually raised on rudely finished buttresses and furnished with peculiar and characteristic lockplates. The locks were often of the greatest richness and intricately wrought, sometimes requiring several keys to open them. Chests of late Gothic days were finished entirely in the richest flamboyant ironwork, never perhaps with quite the refinement and knowledge of architectural forms as seen in France, but often displaying more originality.

A splendid chest in repoussé is in the Madrid Museum. It is Byzantine in character though whether it is as early as this would imply is difficult to say. It may have been made in Gothic days under the inspiration of some richly carved Moorish ivory box. Both the sides and the gabled lid are divided into small panels of uniform size, which are filled with charming little figures of ladies, knights afoot and mounted, dragons, etc. Figure 81 is a velvet-covered trunk with rich iron fittings in the Hispanic collection. Figure 82 is a small beautifully tooled leather box with iron fittings.

CANDELABRAS, BRAZIERS, AND OTHER SMALL OBJECTS

Another medieval object interesting to the student of ironwork is the *candelero* of which several Catalan examples are illustrated. These modest utensils, bespeaking the relative luxury of wax candles instead of olive oil for lighting interiors, were used from the beginning of the eleventh century in churches and homes north of the Ebro. The Museum of Vich has a large and diversified collection in which the development of the candelabra may be traced. The oldest form is based on the Roman oil lamp and has a basin or drip plate at the bottom. Later the central stem or pricket was augmented by branches holding sockets for smaller candles, and the whole was mounted on three spreading feet, as in the eleventh century example (Figure 83). In the later (Figure 84), the base has become a square pan, with central and corner prickets. These two are small, about fourteen and seventeen inches high, and were used on the table;

FIG. 74. CHEST LOCK WITH CANOPY.
Late XV Century.
Hispanic Society of America.
Height 8 in., width 6½ in.   No. 112.

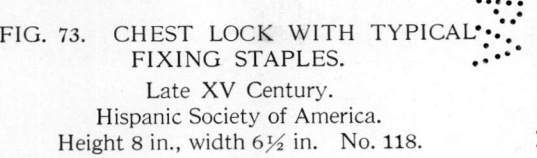

FIG. 73. CHEST LOCK WITH TYPICAL
FIXING STAPLES.
Late XV Century.
Hispanic Society of America.
Height 8 in., width 6½ in.   No. 118.

EASTON PUBLIC LIBRARY
EASTON PA

GOTHIC HARDWARE AND UTENSILS 63

but Figures 85 and 86 are five and six feet high, and were used in churches. The making of candeleros was such a thriving business that very many artizans were engaged in it and thus, though the type of the object changed but little throughout the Gothic period, the manner of adorning it was full of variety and fancy. In the more mountainous regions the smith

FIG. 83.
TABLE CANDELERO PATTERNED AFTER THE ROMAN.
In the museum at Vich.
XI Century. Height 14 in.

FIG. 84.
TABLE CANDELERO.
Catalan. In the Museum at Vich.
XV Century. Height 17 in.

slashed and hammered his central pricket out into the lily form already seen in the crestings of the Barcelona rejas; down in the towns, where there is more suspicion of French or Flemish influence, the crown form of Figure 86 was most in vogue. This shape, very large and without any central standard, was also made to hang from the ceiling by massive chains, and is the prototype of many modern pendant chandeliers in brass and bronze. Among smaller pieces in the Vich Museum, known as *candeleros de mesa*, a number bear traces of having been gilded; this was

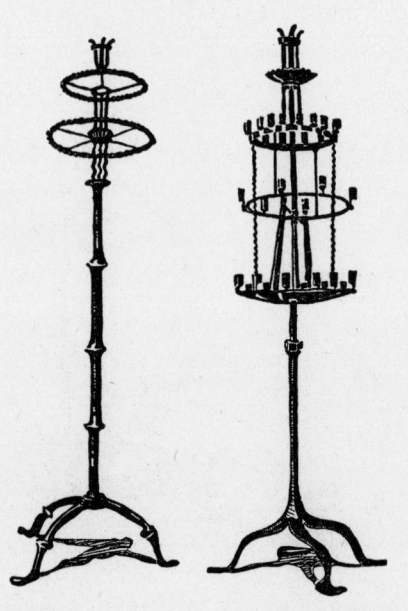

FIG. 85.
ECCLESIASTICAL CANDELABRA.
Catalan. In the Museum at Vich.
XIII Century.
Height 5 ft. 6 in.

FIG. 86.
ECCLESIASTICAL CANDELABRA.
Catalan. In the Museum at Vich.
XV Century.
Height 5 ft.

done not only to produce a rich effect but also to make rusting impossible. In Aragón, as late as the seventeenth century, the tall form of Figure 87 was still plentifully produced, but with the difference that the central stem was generally twisted — a peculiarity seldom met with outside this province. *Hacheros*,

FIG. 76. LOCK AND HASP.
Elaborate Mudéjar design.   XVII Century.
Hispanic Society of America.
Extreme width of hasp 14 in.   No. 114.

EASTON PUBLIC LIBRARY
EASTON PA

or torch holders, were similar to candeleros, but without feet. Attached permanently to the wall was another type of torch holder — the stiff forearm with clenched fist grasping a socket.

Of as widespread use as the candlestick from which the interior was lighted was the *brazero* by which it was heated — or rather, by which the icy, vault-like atmosphere of stone dwellings was slightly mitigated. For the Spanish brazier the classic tripod form was not favored; instead, a circular or polygonal table-like standard with an opening in the top to receive

FIG. 89. BRAZIER ON WHEELS.
Catalan. XIV Century.

the dish of charcoal was used. The more prosperous Spanish families had a two-storied affair accomodating a chafing dish below for foot-warming and an upper one for the hands. This type was usually of generous circumference, so that it was possible for several people to draw up a chair to it as at table. Not always was the entire frame of iron; more often it was of wood, rimmed or entirely covered with sheet metal fastened down with decorative nails. Figure 88 in the Hispanic Society's collection is an excellent example of the all-iron stand, and dates from the early seventeenth century; its additional iron supports of the foot-rest, between the four legs, leave no doubt as to whether this lower feature was utilized. Far more numerous were the low brazeros with one dish set in a small stand of solid wood or a skeleton stand of iron. These were either left on the floor

FIG. 90. IRON FIRE-DOG.
Catalan. XV Century.

or lifted on the table, and still form the only heating apparatus in rural Spain.

A style of Spanish brazier but little seen to-day is the rectangular receptacle mounted on wheels and pulled about, from which the altar boys filled their incense holders. It was used mostly in the chilly

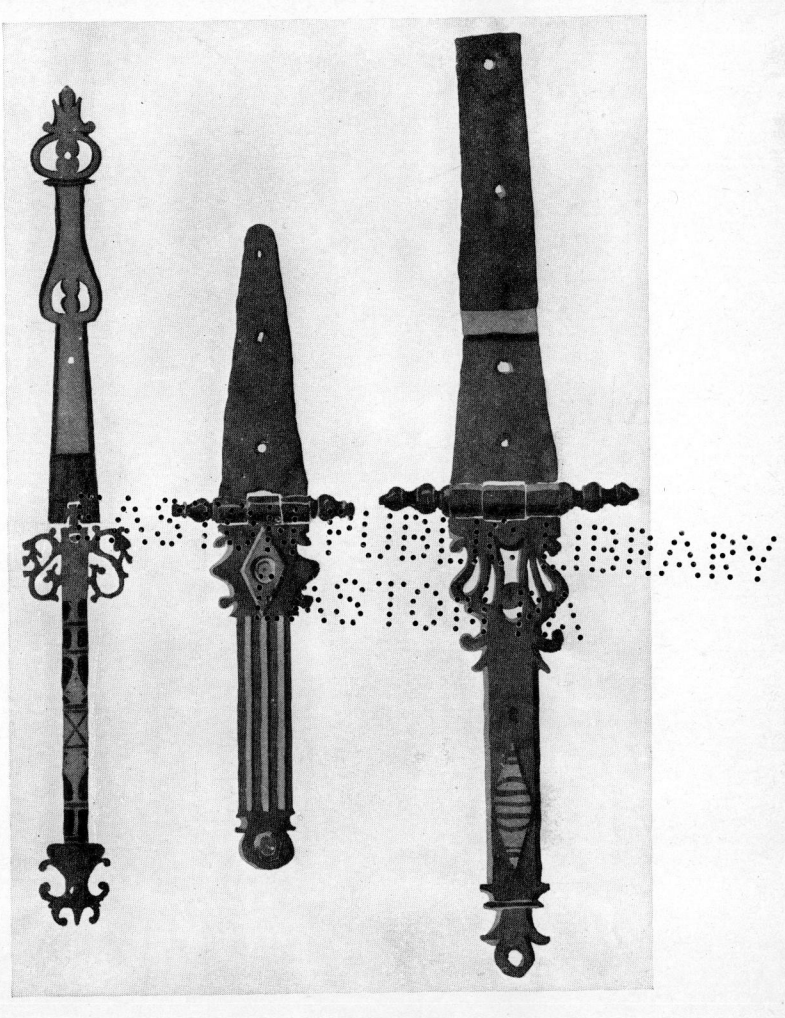

FIG. 77. CHEST HASP.
Late XVI Century.   Hispanic Society of America.
Length 16 in.   No. 129.
FIG. 78. CHEST HASP.
Typical of the XVII Century.   Hispanic Society of America.
Length 12 in.   No. 127.
FIG. 79. CHEST HASP.
Typical of the XVII Century.   Hispanic Society of America.
Length 18 in.   No. 119.

EASTON PUBLIC LIBRARY
EASTON PA

GOTHIC HARDWARE AND UTENSILS 67

vestry-rooms of churches. Figure 89 is an example of one of these Catalan grates or cribs of the fourteenth century belonging to Barcelona Cathedral.

Owing to the general absence of chimneys in Spanish houses, Gothic hearth accessories, demanded so

FIG. 91. GUARD AND FIRE-DOGS.
Museo del Greco, Toledo.

plentifully from French and English smiths, were practically unknown except in Catalonia. Even there the chimney was rare, while in the rest of Spain very few palaces were furnished with it until the eighteenth century. In the Louvre is a Spanish fire screen, purely Flemish in character in its five pierced Gothic panels, but with a Mudéjar cresting and Castilian turrets at

68 GOTHIC HARDWARE AND UTENSILS

the base, Figure 91 shows a beautiful Renaissance chimney-piece from the house of the painter El Greco in Toledo. The broad iron guard of no particular epoch is nevertheless interesting with its tall twisted end supports, opening out to hold ladles or other kitchen utensils, for to this day the Spanish meal is prepared at the one and only fireplace in the house.

FIG. 81. ARCON, OR TRUNK WITH IRON FITTINGS
Hispanic Society of America.
Length 4 ft. 2 in., height 2 ft.

FIG. 82. SMALL LEATHER STRONG BOX.
Hispanic Society of America.
Length 17 in., height 11½ in.

EASTON PUBLIC LIBRARY
EASTON PA

FIG. 88. BRAZIER IN TWO STORIES.
XVII Century.
Hispanic Society of America. No. 164.
Height 3 ft., 2 in.

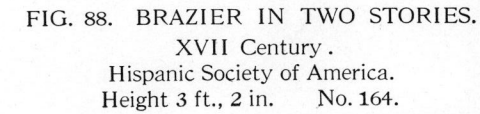

FIG. 87. ECCLESIASTICAL CANDELABRA.
XVI Century.
Hispanic Society of America. No. 163.
Height 5 ft.

EASTON PUBLIC LIBRARY
EASTON PA

IV
THE DEVELOPMENT OF THE RENAISSANCE REJA

SPINDLES AND COLONNETTES

THAT the term Plateresque was chosen to designate early Spanish Renaissance architecture because it was ornamented in the minute manner of the silversmith's (or platero's) art, would in itself indicate that metalwork was both popular and respected at the time. The influence of fifteenth century Italian art penetrated into Spain about 1500, the first Plateresque buildings being the hospitals in Toledo and in Santiago which Enrique de Egas of Flanders built. As Gothic was in a thriving state when rich ecclesiastics began importing the Renaissance, it did not immediately succumb to the new style. Gothic buildings continued to be erected, and those in Renaissance still borrowed many Gothic features; the result was one of charm and novelty. This is especially true in the decorative accessories where some very effective hybrid forms may be encountered. That it was the superficial side of the Italian Renaissance that appealed most to the Spaniards was natural for they had had long association with Moorish art, which, as has been explained, was ornamental rather than structural. Wherever Spanish Renaissance is encountered it is invariably sumptuous, for Spain in this century enjoyed an unprecedented expansion of wealth, power, and territory; and as the activity of the smith generally reflected the condition of his country, Spanish ironwork became a thing of unsurpassed grandeur. It remained largely Gotico-florido during the beginning of the Renaissance or Plateresque period; but when, after a time, the new style dominated with its rich architectural treatments and its unhesitating use of the human figure (previously rare in iron), the smith became a magician. What he now produced was, to quote the great English authority, J. Starkie Gardner, "of so grand and impressive a character as to confound all our previous conceptions of the capabilities of the material. The limits that its stubborn nature and the technical difficulties of the craft seem to impose are disregarded and, in contemplating the colossal rejas in the great Spanish cathedrals, it is hard to realize that effects in iron must be got swiftly by the hammer and punch while the iron is hot, or tediously by the file, chisel, and drill while it is cold."

The adoption of the Renaissance spindle as the upright member has already been mentioned under the heading "Development of the Vertical Bar." This spindle was not the result of a gradual evolution of form, but suddenly appears as a perfected unit in the reja, the only difference between the earliest and latest examples being in the amount of ornament lavished on them. "The happy idea of the replacement of plain or twisted rectangular bars by spindled

FIG. 92. RENAISSANCE BAND IN REPOUSSÉ.
Perforated.   Early XVI Century.   Hispanic Society of America.
Width 5 in.   No. 157.

FIG. 93. RENAISSANCE BAND IN REPOUSSÉ.
XVI Century.   Hispanic Society of America.
Width 6 in.   No. 148.

FIG. 94. RENAISSANCE BAND IN REPOUSSÉ.
Middle XVI Century.   Hispanic Society of America.
Width 6 in.   No. 146.

FIG. 95. RENAISSANCE BAND IN REPOUSSÉ.
Late XVI Century.   Hispanic Society of America.
Width 7 in.   No. 144.

EASTON PUBLIC LIBRARY
EASTON PA

balusters, which led to such important departures, must evidently have been an individual idea, due, no doubt, to one of the great masters who changed their style with the times, like Friar Francés of Salamanca." (J. Starkie Gardner.) The spindle, no matter what its dimensions, was always forged from the solid; the longest ones weighed from two hundred and fifty to three hundred pounds. It was made, presumably, by beating out a bar of the required length, and then in order to obtain the proper section, certain portions were diminished in diameter by excessive beating and the greater diameter was secured by the welding of additional metal, a feat which can be accomplished in iron only. Besides the great muscular effort of welding together so many pieces, the spindle required infinite skill and patience to avoid a ragged unsightly joining. The spindle was further worked with careful regard to perfect symmetry, until it became in the latest days almost as mechanically perfect as the turned baluster. A graceful outline alone did not long content the rejero, for he soon set to work to devise some sort of surface decoration for his new form, and decided to envelop the bulging portion with leaf forms chiseled while cold. This treatment was at first crude, as in the separate spindles, Nos. 165, 166, 167, and 168 in the Hispanic collection, but later it acquired all the graceful modeling of sheet repoussé work and marked the decorative climax of the spindle. Afterwards when all restraint was lost and the foliated enrichments almost covered the entire length and were heavily gilded besides, the usual weakening effect of over-ornamentation is perceptible, as in the door reja of the library of Salamanca University (Figure 115).

Another innovation in vertical members of rejas was the pilaster or column. It will be remembered that in the Gothic Barcelona grilles no one upright received any special accentuation, not even the end bars; for the featuring of certain motifs and members is a purely Renaissance idea. We see it first practiced in the attenuated pilasters of the Sigüenza example (Figure 97), which are used to frame the gates within the reja and are carried on clear to the top. Like all early pilasters they are solid, and in this case about three inches square, and their four sides chiseled with Renaissance ornament. From this modest beginning the pilaster grew into the massive proportions of the square column seen in the detail from Granada (Figure 25). The massiveness here was, however, merely simulated, for the square column was in reality a stout oaken core, sheathed in iron plates; but its proportions served nevertheless to give great architectural emphasis to the whole. Columns, large or small, were generally of the Corinthian order since its attenuation and ornamentation were best adapted to iron. In no sense was it a mere copy of stone Corinthian, but was interpreted in the spirit of metal, from which it drew a sympathetic response which the ironworkers of the eighteenth century classic revival in England and France failed utterly to obtain. On the larger iron-cased Spanish column all the popular

FIG. 96. NAVE OF BURGOS CATHEDRAL.
Showing the importance of the reja in Spanish churches.

EASTON PUBLIC LIBRARY
EASTON PA

forms of Renaissance decoration may be found embossed. The work was extremely delicate in detail and shows that, if the artizan were not actually a silversmith, he was at least far more conversant with *orfèvrerie* than with the vanishing methods of iron smithing. This fact is again apparent in the introduction of many finely modeled medallion portraits in repoussé (frieze of Toledo coro reja, Figure 100); even large compositions were executed by the same process as may be seen in Figure 102.

OTHER RENAISSANCE FEATURES

Along with the foregoing, the extensive use of heraldry, of broad ornamented friezes, and of the human figure complete the most salient additions in Renaissance ironwork. Armorial bearings were mentioned in connection with the Gotico-florido period. Renaissance rejeros developed them into a more highly important motif. While the grille still remained of medium height, that is under twenty-five feet, the blazon of its donor occupied the center of the cresting; but later when the whole composition grew more lofty, it was dropped down into the body of the grille. Coats of arms were colored and gilded (see page 38), a treatment carried to a point of great magnificence in the detail of the reja in the Royal Chapel at Granada (Figure 105).

The introduction of an ornamental horizontal member to break up the severe verticality of the early Gothic reja has already been discussed. In Renaissance days not merely one, but two or three of these made their appearance in the same composition and assumed the importance of a frieze, thus responding to the increased height and importance of the verticals (Figure 101). In Gothic days bands had generally been of open work; those now under consideration were more often solid and beaten in repoussé. Figures 92 to 95 are examples taken from small rejas. The ornamented band was not confined to the reja but was used in diminutive scale and beautifully worked on chests and caskets.

The human figure is seen everywhere in Renaissance ironwork, a profusion which may be explained as a reaction against the ban put upon its use in art by the Moors. George Street, in the description already cited of the Pamplona Gothic grille, marvels at the facility with which the figures "are all elaborately hammered up out of the solid." But these were of minute size — about the same as seen on Gothic knockers — and were so rarely attempted in that period that they may well have astonished Street who, being interested only in Gothic, did not examine the really startling productions of later days when human figures "are not merely introduced singly or in pairs, but in multitudes; and the master ironworkers have not hesitated to attempt even the portrayal of scenes and historical events. The character and execution of this figure work make it impossible to believe that those who produced it were only smiths, and we find, in fact, that the masters who signed their names to such magnificent productions are spoken of by contemporaries as sculptors and architects and were

FIG. 97. REJA OF THE CAPILLA DE SANTA LIBRADA.
Sigüenza Cathedral. Early XVI Century.

EASTON PUBLIC LIBRARY
EASTON PA

in two or three instances in holy orders. They were indeed artists of the highest rank."

This extraordinary figure work, however, was not always forged from the solid; for aside from the question of labor, its weight alone when posed in a cresting would have made it impracticable. It was therefore beaten out of two thin sheets of iron, one the front and one the back, and these riveted together to form the round, as may be detected in the amorini of the Casa Pilatos reja (Figure 119). This particular kind of repoussé work required great skill to maintain uniform thickness in the modeled sheet of metal — a process known as "moving the metal along" by blows in such a way that the greatest projection required by the patterning should be of the same thickness as its lowest point of relief. This special knack is practically lost to-day.

Italy, home of the Renaissance, produced but little ironwork in that great period, and nothing like the same understanding of architecturalizing it was ever grasped by her artizans. Because a few smaller objects, notably the Strozzi lanterns in Florence, show a glimpse of it, and because in this last are to be seen "cornices, columns and capitals in iron," Vasari wrote enthusiastically that its artificer "was without an equal in the past and probably not to be excelled in the future." Had this appreciative biographer lived in Spain where the works which excelled the Strozzi lanterns were so numerous, he would have left us volumes concerning the Spanish rejeros. As it is, however, their names are mostly unknown. From the

"Diccionario de los Artífices Sevillanos" by Gestoso y Perez, we learn the names of a very few. Scanning these, one finds the rejeros were often silversmiths, armorers and architects as well. Even without much data on the subject, a critic could not but feel that they were artists of broad training, for in every important work we find, as in the best work of any medium, constructiveness paramount and ornamentation subservient. It is recorded that several of these Renaissance rejas were felt to be so important that the builder was chosen by competition as in architectural works; and that elaborate drawings and even complete models in wood had to be prepared. Our knowledge of these conditions, scant though it is, enables us to understand the excellences in their designing.

It has been mentioned that the Renaissance was brought into Spain at a moment of great national expansion. Granada had fallen and all Spain was Christian. New churches were built and in these, and also in the old thirteenth century Gothic creations of Fernando el Santo, the noble families of the land vied with each other in dedicating and furnishing special sepulchral chapels which, containing magnificent tombs and costly offerings, necessitated the erection of adequate rejas. Throughout the sixteenth century there was no busier artizan in all Spain than the rejero. Besides religious zeal, another stimulus was given him by the important decision of the Spanish clergy to make a change in the interior arrangement of their churches, this change being the removal

FIG. 99. REJA OF THE CAPILLA DE SANTA MAGDELENA.
Cloisters of Tarragona Cathedral. Early XVI Century.

FIG. 98. REJA OF THE PUERTA DEL CARDO. León Cathedral. Late XV Century.

EASTON PUBLIC LIBRARY
EASTON PA

FIG. 100. REJA OF THE CORO.
Toledo Cathedral. 1549.

EASTON PUBLIC LIBRARY
EASTON PA

of the priests' choir (coro) from the east end down into the nave of the cathedral, where it faced the high altar (altar mayor or capilla mayor). This was an endeavor to get back to the arrangement of the early Christian basilica as can be still seen in San Clemente in Rome. The change, inaugurated in Spain in the early sixteenth century, placed the coro where it blocked up the nave in a way that must have distressed the architect, but which gave a great opportunity to the rejero; for the coro reja, now opposite to that of the altar mayor, was made to correspond to it in height and grandeur. Those of the side chapels were but little less imposing, and in the case of certain noted families like the Constable of Castile's, their chapel reja even surpasses that of the high altar. Figure 96, merely a corner glimpse of the vast Cathedral of Burgos, shows how reja followed reja in the great Spanish churches.

In reja-making, as in architecture, the transition from Gothic to Plateresque was gradual; but the architect soon outstripped the ironworker, and buildings of purest Renaissance were being erected while the ironworker was still experimenting with tentative Renaissance ornament. There was, however, this difference; that the architect received his forms fully developed from Italy, whereas the rejero, having no Italian prototype in iron to study, needed time to work out his problems. Whatever he grasped of the new art was first expressed in the ornament rather than the form of the reja; so that along with twisted Gothic bars and the simplest horizontal members, we find classic details such as amorini, palmettes, wreaths, festoons, shells, and egg-and-dart mouldings, all crudely worked at first.

One of the first difficulties that confront artizans in the working out of any new style is the lack of appropriate tools. As an art develops through experience so does the fashioning of adequate tools. The new details practiced in the Renaissance — amorini, arabesques, and floral forms — were vastly different from the geometric perforations of the Gothic, and intricate though these last were, the tools required for them would not suffice for the new forms. The ironworker, with such tools as he had at the beginning of the Renaissance period, roughed out the patterns while the iron was still hot, and afterward, when the metal was cold, went over it with finer tools to pick out the detail. But these first attempts were crude, and examples are often found in the transitional period where wonderful facility is exhibited in the execution of some rich flamboyant ornamentation, while simpler Renaissance forms in the same grille and undoubtedly by the same man are worked with childish awkwardness, due as much to lack of proper tools as to lack of experience. As these were perfected the execution lost somewhat in charm until to-day, with manifold and over-perfected implements, a cold precision is the inevitable result. To demonstrate the truth of this the modern plasterer's equipment was recently taken away from a group of workmen and the Elizabethan kit handed them instead. With this they were asked to do their best. The finished work, offered by

FIG. 101. REJA OF THE CAPILLA MAYOR.
Sevilla Cathedral. 1518–33.

EASTON PUBLIC LIBRARY
EASTON PA

them with many an apology, savored of much of the charm of early English plastering and was thoroughly satisfactory. The same experiment might be profitably tried on the modern ironworker.

V
RENAISSANCE CHURCH REJAS

TO follow chronologically the evolution or even the erecting of important Renaissance rejas would be impossible, not only because cathedral records are hard to get at but because the evolution was not logical. In certain great centers of progress it went ahead rapidly; in remoter spots where, nevertheless, chapels and rejas were built with equal devotion, the new style came late and only partially. It will suffice to mention a certain number of the larger cities where reja-making was carried on most vigorously and to give a few examples from each.

SIGÜENZA, LEÓN, TARRAGONA

In Sigüenza Cathedral, one of the most magnificent late Romanesque structures in Spain, there is much early Renaissance ironwork; this because the bishop holding the see in the early sixteenth century added a late Gothic cloister and, in the body of the cathedral itself, some fine Renaissance chapels. Two of the cloister rejas have already been mentioned as illustrating Gotico-florido (Figures 31 and 32). That of the chapel of Santa Librada in the transept of the cathedral may be quoted as a very early Renaissance example (Figure 97). Surrounded as it is by Plat-

FIG. 103. REJA OF THE CORO.
Sevilla Cathedral. 1519.

eresque stonework, it bears out the remark previously made that the architect was more advanced in the new forms than the ironworker. In the stonework both ornamentation and structural details such as the arch, impost, and spandrel, are fully developed; while in the reja the form is still medieval, and, viewed from a distance in the dim interior where its new surface decoration is not discernible, it gives every indication of belonging to the earlier period; but near at hand, the little square columns flanking the gate (which in this instance are solid) are seen to be covered with Renaissance arabesques, and to have an appropriate base although not developed sufficiently to have a cap. In the cresting are found, rather bluntly worked out, dolphins and candelabras, so much in vogue later during the High Renaissance; while more Italian details may be seen in the horizontal bands, still flat and unmoulded. Aside from the foregoing superficial Italian treatment, the structural elements are the same as in work done a hundred years before. Within this chapel the much venerated Santa Librada lies in a marble tomb erected in 1530 by Bishop Fadrique de Portugal; this tomb is railed off by a beautiful low iron screen, about eight feet high, which has all the early Renaissance character of the larger work just described, and was probably made by the same unknown rejero.

In León Cathedral, at the Puerta del Cardo (Figure 98) is another reja with Gothic and Renaissance details interspersed, but framed this time in very late Gothic stonework. In the bases of the four shortened spindles one sees Renaissance pedestals filled with pure flamboyant tracery. The spindles of this reja have not yet acquired a capital, but instead are crowned by a curious little scroll indicative of later-day caps and volutes. In the cloister chapel of Santa Magdalena at Tarragona (Figure 99), is a simple reja whose featured lockplate and rather naïve cresting attract attention as indicating touches of the new style.

TOLEDO

In Toledo, which held one of the three grand Gothic cathedrals of Spain and whose bishop was primate of the whole kingdom, the adornment of the church was naturally lavish and unceasing, and records of it are comparatively copious. Among the side chapels and subsidiary buildings with notable rejas may be mentioned the vestry with one at the entrance made in 1494 by "El Maestro Juan Francés, maestro mayor de las armas de hierro en España;" and the Capilla Mozárabe in the southwest tower with another by the same armorer (maestro de armas); the sagrario with chapel rejas by Bartolomé Rodriguez, Luis de Peñafiel, and Francisco de Silva; the Capilla de los Reyes Nuevos, with a screen by Domingo de Céspedes who also made the one for the baptistry and for the Capilla de Reyes Viejos in 1529. Another of his works, that for the coro, is illustrated in Figure 100. This rejero, called "El Maestre Domingo," was born near Toledo but there is no record of where he received his training; his ironwork, however, shows him

FIG. 104. REJA IN THE CAPILLA REAL.
Granada. 1523.

EASTON PUBLIC LIBRARY
EASTON PA

to have imbibed Renaissance ideas and to have been conversant with the allied arts of architecture and sculpture. One of his assistants is known to have been Francisco Bravo.

In the Céspedes reja illustrated, which is twenty-five feet high, his only deviation from strictly Renaissance precepts is the placing of the colonnette directly in the middle, thus creating an even number of bays. Otherwise the composition is built up on purely orthodox principles; — base or pedestal, columns, entablature, and cresting. The spindle baluster only is used, though the same Domingo had made Gothic twisted bars for several of the side chapels. The spindles are very lofty and are uninterrupted by any horizontal motif until they reach the frieze below the cresting. A combination of short spindles and medallion portraits hammered in repoussé make up the unusually interesting frieze; while the cresting, which is composed of candelabra, grotesques, heraldic ornament, and foliation, shows an exquisite feeling for Renaissance. Perhaps the greatest achievement in the reja might be considered the seven large colonnettes, for they are worked from the solid with a delicacy that one would hardly believe possible in iron. This whole reja was silvered and gilded and must have been most sumptuous and costly; but when Napoleon's plundering troops were reported approaching the city, the silver was hidden under a coat of black paint which has never been removed. Coro and altar mayor were both given out to competition in 1540 by the Cathedral Chapter. Alonzo de Covarrubias, one of the greatest Renaissance architects, acted as adviser to the chapter and chose Domingo's design for the coro and Francisco de Villalpando's for the altar. Both works were finished in 1549, their making having kept a tribe of smiths busy for seven years. It is on record that Domingo made a complete model in wood before starting his work.

The other successful competitor, Villalpando (maker of the bronze doors of the Puerta de los Leones), created for the capilla mayor a reja as magnificent as Domingo's but inferior in design and somewhat too exuberant in spirit for such monumentality. However, despite the incongruity and confusion of the detail, much of it is very beautifully wrought. The whole is crowned by a colossal crucifix once silvered and gilded. This same artist made the two beautiful Renaissance pulpits in bronze at either side of the capilla mayor, and also the charming little railing enclosing the celebrated "Virgén de la Blanca" within the coro. That he was well versed in the Italian art and language is proved by his having translated into Spanish Serlio's great work on architecture.

SEVILLA

Sevilla Cathedral, the largest Gothic church in Christendom and one of the richest, contains, naturally, an abundance of fine rejería. The church was built throughout the fifteenth century and its rejas, added after the structure was completed, are therefore Renaissance. There is even one, that of the Capilla Real, finished as late as 1773. Of the numerous

FIG. 105. ARMS OF FERDINAND AND ISABELLA
AND THEIR GRANDSON CHARLES V.
Reja in the Capilla Real, Granada. 1523.

EASTON PUBLIC LIBRARY
EASTON PA

FIG. 106. REJA OF THE CAPILLA DE LA PRESENTACIÓN.
Burgos Cathedral. Middle XVI Century.

EASTON PUBLIC LIBRARY
EASTON PA

examples enclosing side chapels those to the Capillas de la Gamba and de la Antigua are very beautiful, with armorial bearings and figure work representing the events after which the chapels are named. Even finer are those of the Concepción and the Anunciación. The vestry reja was made by Fernando Prieto in 1510; and that of the library of the cathedral in 1527 by Pedro de Andino, father of the celebrated Cristóbal. Around the tomb of Cardinal Cervantes is a magnificent verja made in 1537 by Antonio de Palencia and Juan Delgado.

The high altar, or capilla mayor, unlike those in most Spanish churches, is very open in appearance because of having rejas instead of masonry on three of its four sides. These side screens, while of great richness, are treated subordinately to that at the front and are the work of Sancho Muñez, a master rejero of Cuenca who started them in 1518. Their average height is nearly thirty-five feet, the lower half treated with twisted bars and the upper with a series of ornamental bands. They are gilded to accord with the capilla mayor and coro. Muñez was helped by Bartolomé of Jaén (of whom more will be heard later), Juan de Yepes, and Diego de Idrobo. As this is about the time that Friar Francisco de Salamanca was starting the main reja of the same chapel, these various rejeros, to judge from the harmony between the front and sides, must have collaborated wisely.

The two mightiest Plateresque achievements in Sevilla Cathedral are the rejas to the coro and capilla mayor; the latter (Figure 101) was made by the celebrated friar Francisco de Salamanca between 1518 and 1533. The composition is divided horizontally by elaborate openwork friezes into two stages and cresting; and vertically by well emphasized colonnettes into five bays, the central being widest to accommodate the grand double gates. A feeling of increased height is given to the reja by carrying the colonnettes through with varying form from base to cresting. The friar's uprights are all spindles and at each side five of these are almost invisibly hinged into a gate that gives access to the splendid iron pulpits. Both the friezes are remarkable achievements, the upper one especially with its fine medallions and arabesques; but the surpassing portion is the cresting which abounds with angelic figures within scrolls and separated from each other by tall candelabras in line with the colonnettes below. The center of the frieze is occupied by a magnificent embossed panel of the Entombment; the solidity of this motif contrasts very effectively with the openness of the rest of the work (Figure 102).

This Dominican monk-rejero was one of the greatest of Spain's numerous iron artists. He was at first a Carthusian, an inmate of the monastery of Miraflores near Burgos which contains fine late Gothic specimens of his work; later he went to the Chartreuse of Paular near Segovia where he made another splendid reja. Ceán Bermudez says, among interesting details concerning him, "That his many virtues were praised by the canons of Sevilla; that he willingly accepted from time to time wheat instead of ducats; and that

FIG. 107. REJA OF THE CAPILLA DEL CONDESTABLE.
Burgos Cathedral. 1523.

EASTON PUBLIC LIBRARY
EASTON PA

his industry was amazing, for with all his reja-making he found time to repair the great clock of the Giralda and devise an ingenious alarm for arousing the cathedral bell ringers." He was still working in Sevilla as late as 1547, having meanwhile been employed in Guadalupe and in the cathedral and university of his

FIG. 102. PANEL OF THE ENTOMBMENT, REJA OF THE CAPILLA MAYOR.
Sevilla Cathedral.

native city, Salamanca. The Sevilla pulpits to be described later are also by his hand.

Sancho or Pancho Muñez of Cuenca, who made the side rejas of the capilla mayor, also made that of the coro in 1519 (Figure 103), which one could hardly say is less grand than the friar's work facing it. Sancho's, although he never overcame his predilection for the twisted bar beloved of Gothicists, must be classed as Plateresque. That he designed it in sympathy with the friar is evident from the general harmony of their productions. The actual proportions vary in accordance with the tradition that the high altar should have the grander reja; but the feeling of both shows a studied agreement. The twisted bars composing the body of the coro screen are surmounted by a tier of short Renaissance spindles; and, instead of being uniformly twisted, alternately spiral toward each other. Their expanse is marked off into five bays by six-inch-square pilasters — the usual wooden-core sheathed in richly embossed iron. The beautiful little Corinthian capitals crowning them are most intricately worked out, not along the lines of stone Corinthian but into a truly wrought-iron interpretation; and the delicately twisted volutes are forged from tongue-shaped pieces as if rolling themselves unaided like the sheet of parchment which tradition tells us inspired the form. Horizontal courses and cornices are beaten out of sheet metal and make, along with the pilasters, a lavish display of the embosser's skill. They are fashioned from metal one-sixteenth of an inch thick, kept rigid by interior transverse tie-pieces. The gilt inscription above the spindles is effectively backgrounded by vermillion. The frieze is three feet high, composed of Renaissance scrolls and wreaths; and above this again is the most resplendent portion of all — a cresting representing the tree of Jesse. Each

FIG. 108. ESCALERA DORADA OR GOLDEN
STAIRWAY.
Burgos Cathedral. 1519.

of the personages composing it is framed in a circle of foliation and is a masterpiece of figure-work in iron. A facetious innovation in the cresting, and one serving a practical purpose as well, is the little bell frame at either end. These are charming in design and execution and have the value of solidity as end motifs to such an imaginative cresting. One of the quaint details recorded of Sancho Muñez's sojourn in Sevilla is that he "lived in the house of Canon Martin Navarro to whom the Cathedral Chapter regularly paid his board."

GRANADA

In the Capilla Real, or Royal Chapel, which communicates with Granada Cathedral, is to be found one of the most sumptuous rejas in all Spain (Figure 104). That there is so little ironwork of artistic value in the cathedral itself is due to the late date of its erection. It was started in 1523 (after the completion of the Capilla Real) and though consecrated in 1561 was still incomplete at that date. By this time Spain was growing poor and rejas were becoming less important; but fortunately for Granada the Royal Chapel, designed by Enrique de Egas in 1506 for Charles V, was completed in time to give Maestre Bartolomé of Jaén opportunity to build the reja separating the royal monuments of Ferdinand and Isabella from the rest of the chapel. Appreciating his opportunity Maestre Bartolomé designed a grille of such stupendous proportions that nothing comparable to it was ever attempted elsewhere. Two solid unpierced friezes divide the composition horizontally into three diminishing stages of thirteen, seven, and five feet respectively. In the first of these the tall twisted bars break into quatrefoils and masques (Figure 25), in the next into leaf work and cherubims, and in the third to leaf work alone. Vertically the screen is divided into five parts by massive square columns beautifully embossed and further adorned in the upper stages by statuettes and canopies. The embossed plates, hardly over one-sixteenth of an inch thick, are applied and riveted to an oak core. But the greatest achievement is, as usual, the cresting, here made up of ten biblical scenes containing thirty figures more than half life size. It is a story in iron told as freely as the frescoist would have proceeded on a given wall space. A conventional arrangement of lofty candelabras connected by rich arabesques finishes off the cresting and the whole is topped by a gigantic crucifix with the Virgin on one side and St. John on the other. The arms of Ferdinand and Isabella and of their grandson Charles V, forming the painted and gilded panel above the gates (Figure 105), may be considered the bravura piece of heraldic ironwork in Spain.

This rejero has already been mentioned as having been employed at Sevilla; it is known also that he worked at Jaén which was probably his native place. It is recorded that he had to petition Charles V for sixteen hundred ducats due him which the Granada Chapter had refused to pay. The royal reja was supposed to have been finished in 1523 but no details

FIG. 109. REJA OF THE CORO.
Palencia Cathedral.
Probably 1555.

EASTON PUBLIC LIBRARY
EASTON PA

can be found as to the length of time spent on it.
It is one of the few signed works in iron, its frieze just
below the blazon containing in raised letters the
words: "Maestre Bartolome me fec."

MAEST
REBA
RTOLO
MEM
EFEC

In the same chapel, but by unknown authors, are
other good rejas. Immediately to the right of the
royal reja is one with good Plateresque detail but
obviously not by Maestre Bartolomé. Here too the
blazon is treated in color and, like its more important
neighbor, has this feature contained in the body of
the work and not, as was the general custom in Renaissance days, in the cresting.

BURGOS

Burgos Cathedral, another of the famous Gothic
trio built by Fernando el Santo in the thirteenth century, presents in the screening of its fifteen chapels
an impressive array of rejería. These cover the field
from early Gothic to waning Renaissance, that of the
coro (Figure 96) being as late as 1602. Figure 106
shows the screen of the Capilla de la Presentación, built
probably by Cristóbal de Andino after 1520. It is
a very typical side-chapel reja built to conform to
a rather high and narrow arch. The cresting, with a
cardinal's blazon supported by huge scrolls as a nu-

cleus of the design, has some nice leaf and repoussé work. In the candelabra-like motifs crowning the colonnettes the design and character of the work is somewhat indicative of the decline which set in shortly after this date.

Behind the presbytery of this cathedral opens the large Capilla del Condestable commenced in the richest Plateresque style for the Constable Don Pedro de Velasco. The splendid reja (Figure 107) at its entrance was built by the same Cristóbal de Andino, architect, sculptor, rejero, and silversmith, whose father has been mentioned as one of the ironworkers in Sevilla Cathedral. Even without accurate data as to Andino's attainments, one glance at it would prove its maker to have been an architect. As in most of the later examples, there is a strong domination of the horizontal members; — a preference for classic principles as opposed to Gothic. To give the composition increased architectural feeling Andino has introduced an innovation in the form of two richly wrought columns standing forward of the general plane and making a total depth of fifteen inches framing the postern gate; while further depth and substantiality are imparted by breaking the cornice over the columns and resting the floriated candelabras of the second stage on this projection. To crown the entire composition the very symbol of architecture, the pediment, has been chosen, and supporting it are two kneeling figures whose sophisticated naïveté might well be the envy of modern artists. The author of this work happens to be one of the several rejeros

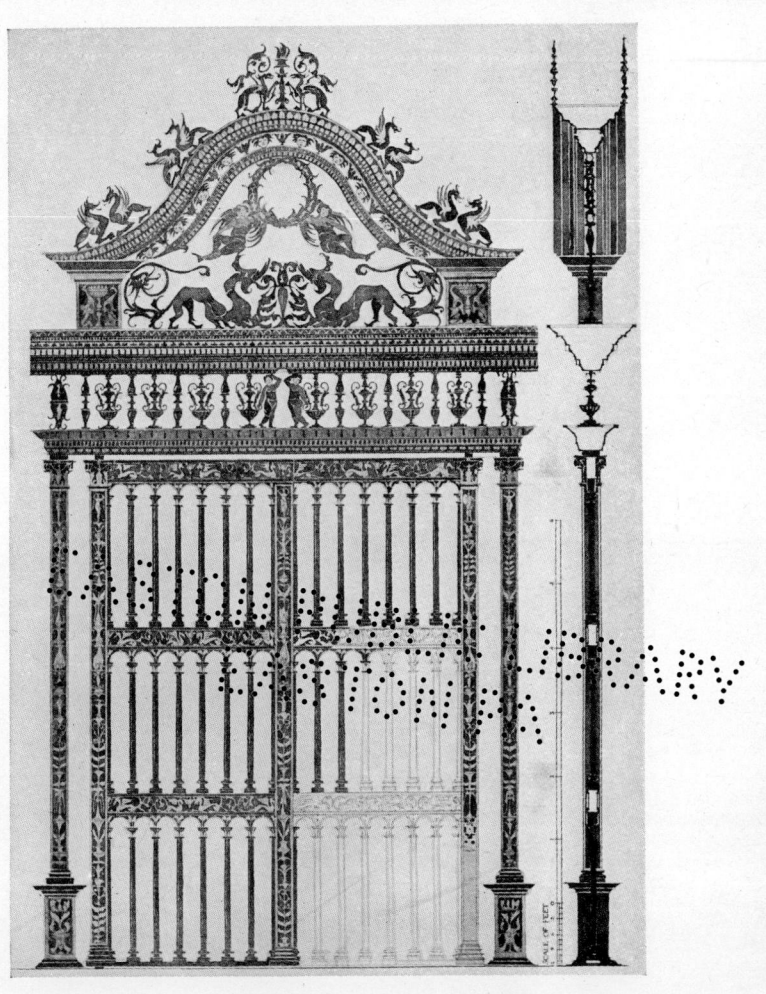

FIG. 110. REJA OF A SIDE CHAPEL.
Cuenca Cathedral.
Middle XVI Century.

EASTON PUBLIC LIBRARY
EASTON PA

FIG. 111. REJA OF A SIDE CHAPEL.
Segovia Cathedral.
Late XVI Century.

EASTON PUBLIC LIBRARY
EASTON PA

about whom some personal data have been preserved. His work commanded a great praise during his lifetime, for a contemporary wrote of it: "All who wish their work to breathe the spirit of authority and to pass without rebuke should follow, like Cristóbal Andino, ancient precept, in that his works have greater beauty and elegance than any I have seen before. If this, you think, be not the case, look at that reja he is making for my lord the Constable, which reja is well known to be superior to all others in the kingdom." This work is signed under the pediment, "Ab Andino." Other works by the talented Cristóbal de Andino are in the capilla mayor and the Capilla de San Pedro in Palencia Cathedral; also a peculiar and extremely architecturalized one in Medina de Rioseco, a small town between Palencia and Valladolid. In 1540 he had the disappointment of competing unsuccessfully for the screens and pulpits of Toledo Cathedral.

Burgos Cathedral contains, besides its many notable rejas, another marvel of the ironworker's art in the shape of its famous "Escalera Dorada" — a double flight of fifty-nine steps in marble and stone, with a marvelous wrought iron balustrade richly gilded (Figure 108). The church, being built on sloping ground, has entrances at various levels, the northwest portal being some twenty-five feet above the nave floor; this difference necessitated a staircase to conduct to the north transept. The problem was solved by building the Escalera Dorada, designed by Diego de Siloe in 1519 and thought to have been executed by Cristóbal de Andino. The elaborate balustrade wrought in iron and heavily gilded varies in design as it ascends from landing to landing. The lowest stage consists of rich balusters or spindles between which are cupid heads and a dolphin arabesque, while at the landing between the two stages are the arms of Bishop Fonseca, donor of the staircase; the next flight has square posts with portrait medallions and arabesques between. The landing at the top projects, not unlike a rostrum, and is supported on a huge corbel; its rail is divided into ten panels, the two central ones contain portraits of saints enwreathed and the remaining are richly decorated with amorini, wreaths, and scrolls. Certainly nothing more ambitious of its kind was ever undertaken and one regrets that the staircase has fallen into disuse due to the violent draughts which compelled the closing of the north portal to which it conducts.

PALENCIA

South of Burgos lies Palencia whose cathedral was also enriched by the works of Andino. Earlier than his contributions, however, are the many Gothic and Gotico-florido rejas in the side chapels. These show a strong Flemish influence — a florid use of sheet iron foliations cut and riveted to their stems rather than beaten out as in the Spanish manner. This influence can be traced to the fact that Palencia's bishop, Fonseca, having been appointed special ambassador to the Low Countries by Ferdinand and Isabella, came back laden down with Flemish tapestries and pictures,

FIG. 112. REJA OF THE CORO.
Plasencia Cathedral. 1604.

EASTON PUBLIC LIBRARY
EASTON PA

and followed by a whole train of Flemish artizans. This northern influence had passed away at the period now under consideration, and the works of Andino in the capilla mayor, and of Gaspar Rodriguez in the coro, are purest Spanish Renaissance. Andino's is simpler in composition than his Burgos work and consists of two tiers of foliated spindles separated by repoussé bands of ornament in the Italian style, while the towering cresting is composed of candelabra, scrolling, and the blazon so popular with Renaissance rejeros. It is on record that he made this reja in 1520 and was paid fifteen hundred ducats for it by Dean Don Gonzalo Zapata whose arms are in the cresting. The same records speak of a screen made in 1530 for which he received four hundred and thirty ducats, but of just which there is no indication; a certain resemblance between the rejas of the Capilla de San Pedro and of the capilla mayor suggests that both are by the same author. Superior to the reja of the capilla mayor is that of the coro (Figure 109) by Gaspar Rodriguez but long ascribed to Villalpando. Much confusion exists as to the date of this piece of work, 1522, 1555, and 1561 being variously given. The first mentioned may be read twice on the marble base of the reja in an inscription referring to Adrian VI who was in Spain in 1522; but anyone who has studied reja-making would be inclined to reject 1522, as the design gives every indication of having been produced in the High Renaissance. It is pure in quality, free and knowing in composition, and decidedly later than the reja of the capilla mayor at Toledo finished about 1548 by Villalpando. A new feature to be observed here is the admirable way in which the screen is tied in architecturally with its surroundings by means of a marble parapet, a treatment which goes far towards making the ironwork an integral part of the edifice. A condition imposed on both of these Palencian rejeros was that the arms of the prelate who donated them should be incorporated as a decorative motif; this, along with the figures of the four evangelists with their emblems, makes for great richness. The crowning figures are of solid bronze and the entire reja is gilt and painted. Both the capilla mayor and the coro were given out to competition, Andino, Villalpando, and Lopez de Urisarri having competed unsuccessfully against Gaspar Rodriguez. Another rejero employed in the same cathedral was Juan Relojero who in 1512 made the screen for the Capilla de Nuestra Señora de Blanca, donated by the Canon Bartolomé de Palencia, who paid for it with twenty-five thousand maravedis and a quantity of grain.

LESS KNOWN EXAMPLES

Among the remoter towns which were important centers of ironwork in the fifteenth and sixteenth centuries are Cuenca, Segovia, Avila, Guadalupe, Oviedo, Osma, Tortosa, Plasencia, and numerous others long since fallen into decay, but whose churches contain a bewildering array of rejería; among towns which have not fallen into decay, but are making rapid strides at modernizing themselves, Zaragoza, Valencia, Mal-

FIG. 113. PORTION OF A REJA CRESTING.
Northern Spain. Early XVII Century.
Hispanic Society of America. No. 169.

aga, and Cadiz also possess fine examples. Figure 110 illustrates one of the side chapel screens from Cuenca, a town already mentioned as the native place of the great rejero Sancho Muñez, who in 1519 made the coro reja in Sevilla Cathedral. Another Muñez production in Cuenca is the beautiful "Jesse Screen" back of the high altar and so-named from the arch-shaped cresting which contains the tree of Jesse including some very delicately worked figures. The similarity of workmanship between this and Figure 110 would suggest that the same rejero was responsible for both. Andrew Prentice, the first English architect who went into Spain to make a study of Spanish Renaissance, has left several beautiful drawings of these side chapel rejas and also one of the huge screen of the capilla mayor. This last is forty-five feet high and was made in 1517 by Hernando de Arenas. From its comparatively early date and the history of the town it is not surprising to find it reminiscent of Gothic. The body is entirely composed of twisted bars unfeatured except by the four thin pilasters. In these and in the horizontal bands Renaissance asserts itself most emphatically; also the cresting, some twelve feet high in itself, is rich in foliation of the new style, but, like Gothic work, has no particular centralized feature. A later reja, in the Capilla de los Caballeros of the same church, is by the same man and has the date 1526 over the entrance gates. In the nine years that passed between its making and the completion of the capilla mayor, Arenas had learned much about the Renaissance, for the Caballeros composition breaks away from Gothic regularity and is interrupted and accentuated in interesting Renaissance fashion.

Segovia was another town celebrated not only for rejas but for all sorts of smaller objects in iron, and curious balconies may still be seen in the Calle Carmen. Many local productions figured in the famous collection (now dispersed) of the Duque de Segovia. The late Gothic Cathedral has, as might be expected, a number of good screens. The one illustrated (Figure 111) is that of a small reja in the Capilla de Nuestra Señora de la Piedad. While dating from the latter half of the sixteenth century it is still in the best taste and the griffins in the cresting are particularly fine; the scrolls in the lower paneling of the gates, however, are slightly indicative of the coming decline in rejería.

At Osma there are the rejas to the capilla mayor and coro made in 1505 by the famous rejero Juan Francés, as recorded in the inscription: "This work was done by the maestro, one Juan Francés, chief maestro of Toledo." A second reads: "This work was ordered to be made by the most magnificent Don Alonzo de Fonseca in the year 1505." These, like much of the work of this rejero in Toledo, are mixed Gothic and Renaissance in style. The same master made the reja in the capilla mayor of the church of San Justo at Alcalá de Henares.

The admirer of Spanish rejería is saved the saddening spectacle of its decline. By the time Baroque had succeeded Renaissance, Spain was (fortunately for

FIG. 115. ENTRANCE REJA TO LIBRARY.
Salamanca University.
XVI Century.

FIG. 114. GATE REJA LEADING TO STAIRWAY.
Salamanca University.
Early XVI Century.

EASTON PUBLIC LIBRARY
EASTON PA

its reputation in ironwork) too poor to add much embellishment to her cathedrals. Whatever new building was ordered was calculated to make a great display for a limited expenditure, as if thus to hide approaching poverty. With such an object in view, the refinement and dignity of iron naturally made no appeal; so the rejero went his way unaffected by the new extravagances of style and made those latest rejas which, while lacking the spontaneity and rich fancy of earlier productions, are in no sense devoid of artistic merit, and suggest a revival of Grecian forms rather than Baroque. In domestic and civil edifices, where metal accessories on a small scale could be employed, Baroque secured a foothold, and it is here, in the form of balustrades, balconies, and smaller accessories, that one must look for examples of this period.

The last church reja illustrated (Figure 112) is from Plasencia and was made in 1604. It is distinctly precise, unemotional, yet extremely dignified; and while there is nothing decadent in it, still there is much that forecasts a decline. This criticism is justified by the lack of variety in its motifs and, even more noticeably, by the abundance of severe architectural mouldings which are merely uninspired copies from stonework, and may be regarded as a link between the fine forged work of earlier days and modern cast ironwork. In other words, this formal and impressive reja lacks that indefinable something called "touch." It is the work of Juan Bautista Celma, the son, probably, of the Celma who made a beautiful late screen in the Cathedral del Pilar in Zaragoza in 1579.

Figure 113 is a reja cresting from northern Spain in the possession of the Hispanic Society. It is not as late as the work just mentioned, and consists of a central heraldic motif supported by scrolls and candelabra. Its workmanship is of good quality and makes it worth close examination by those interested in sixteenth century methods.

It has often been remarked that the productions of the smith are a gauge of the prosperity of his country. This is undeniably the case with the almost superhuman feats of smithery just described. All were produced during Spain's greatest period of grandeur — after the conquest of the Moor and the discovery of the New World. There was no difficulty in ironwork that the smith did not try to overcome; in fact, he courted difficulties and appears to have actually reveled in his work. By the end of the first half of the sixteenth century about every problem that could ever present itself had been solved; from then on, increasingly rich and imposing effects were obtained (but not always in the same straightforward way) until the erection of sumptuous rejas ceased in the early seventeenth century. That the great development of Spanish rejería was due to any interest and encouragement on the part of contemporaneous monarchs — Charles V and Philip II — is far from likely; for these, in the case of armor, ordered all their superb and costly suits from abroad instead of employing Spanish armorers. Not a single specimen in the

FIG. 118. WINDOW REJA, FAÇADE OF THE UNIVERSITY OF ALCALA.

FIG. 117. TYPICAL FAÇADE WITH WINDOW REJAS.
House in Granada.

EASTON PUBLIC LIBRARY
EASTON PA

FIG. 119. WINDOW REJA, CASA DE PILATOS.
Sevilla.   Middle XVI Century.

EASTON PUBLIC LIBRARY
EASTON PA

Royal Armería of Madrid from this period is of Spanish make. It is, therefor, reasonable to suppose that not to royal patronage, but to the irrepressible exuberance of the people themselves, are due the prodigies of smithing herein described.

VI
SMALLER RENAISSANCE PRODUCTIONS

GATES

OF smaller rejas a number for gates and windows are illustrated which have many of the characteristics of the more monumental church works. Figure 114 is an early example of truly utilitarian aspect and has a simple moulded top with Renaissance scroll above. This gate is in the University of Salamanca at the foot of the famous carved staircase leading from the patio to the library. At the entrance to the latter is another reja (Figure 115) which is the very antithesis of simplicity. It consists merely of a dozen spindles and very rich frieze which swings out with the gates; but its few spindles are wrapped in gilt foliation and the embossed and pierced frieze is most elaborate; in fact, hardly an inch of the whole work but is ornamented, yet it is all so delicately executed and so subservient to the ensemble that its richness is not displeasing. In the Hospital of Santa Cruz, at Toledo, is a fine pair of early sixteenth century exterior gates which stand intact and sturdy after their four centuries of exposure. These gates are of spindles and are crowned by a Renaissance feature of amorini supporting the arms of Cardinal Mendoza. The figures are beaten in two halves from sheet metal and then riveted together.

FIG. 120. WINDOW WITH REJA HOOD.
Toledo. XVI Century.

EASTON PUBLIC LIBRARY
EASTON PA

Figure 116 is a pair of gates in the Hispanic collection dating from the end of the same century. Whereas in earlier work the spindle extended the full height, here and in other late examples the lower portion of

FIG. 116. ENTRANCE GATES.
XVII Century.
Hispanic Society of America.
No. 170.

the composition is taken up by a panel filled with scrolling. The Segovia Cathedral reja (Figure 111) exemplifies this same deviation.

WINDOW REJAS

In Renaissance days, notwithstanding the increased law and order that prevailed in the land, the window reja hardly waned in popularity. Figure 117, a house in Granada, gives an idea of its lavish use. Among the finest examples of the period are those on the University of Alcalá de Henares, a town not far east of Madrid (Figure 118). The rejero is unknown; but one writer has suggested Juan Francés who made a reja for the University Chapel and also the fine low railing around the tomb of Cardinal Cisneros in the Colegiate Church of the same city. The University window motif including the reja as shown in the illustration was a very popular one with Spanish architects throughout the sixteenth century. Seen in the strong sunlight, the iron grille with its accompanying shadow against the yellowish stone adds a note of great decorativeness to the façade of the building. Figure 119 is one of the best known window rejas in all Spain and quite deservedly so. It faces on an interior court of the so-called Casa de Pilatos in Sevilla where it stands out so prominently even in this land of rejas that it must be the work of one of the master rejeros employed in the cathedral of the same city. The records of artizans engaged on ecclesiastical and municipal edifices are scanty enough in Spain, but still more scanty are records pertaining to those who were employed on *casas particulares*. The Pilatos grille carries no trace of preceding styles and was probably executed about 1535. In the two tiers of spindles forming the body of the reja it is the restraint that impresses one as much as the ornament. What little exists is worked with an exquisite nicety, the acanthus motif on the spindles being so delicate

FIG. 122. RENAISSANCE PULPIT.
Avila Cathedral.   Early XVI Century.

EASTON PUBLIC LIBRARY
EASTON PA

that it does not in the least interrupt their graceful outline. The two intermediary bands are decaying owing to the fact that until recently this portion of the house had been long abandoned; but it is to be hoped that they may be saved by the general restoration now in progress. The cresting is an example of the Spanish rejeros' great ability at repoussé. It consists, as in other pieces described, of separate sheets for front and back, beaten to forms, and then riveted together. In portions where the metal has fallen away, one may obtain a good idea of how this work was done.

On the house of the Count of Toledo in Toledo is a more common type of sixteenth century window reja, surrounded in this case by fragments of Moorish work (Figure 120). The whole treatment is much less architectural than in the Sevilla example, for, with the exception of the spindles, the rest of the detail is obtained by working in the flat. The bands are formed of sheet iron ornamented with applied flattened rosettes, while the scroll motif at the top, so dear to window rejeros, is beaten from flat iron strips. The gourd-shaped motifs on the corner are also typical, consisting of a cusped acanthus leaf cut from sheet iron and into which little lilies on long stems are poked. The Mudéjar hood above this reja is supported on good iron brackets and, besides protecting, it adds much to the importance of the feature below. Window rejas, like all other iron accessories, were much affected by the prevailing styles of architecture. Under the severe hand of the

106 SMALLER RENAISSANCE PRODUCTIONS

architect Herrera, whose restrained art was in violent contrast to early Renaissance freedom, the reja was brought down to a point of extreme plainness. By the tendency to work in flat expanses of metal and to duplicate stone mouldings, it lost the charm of iron-

FIG. 121. WINDOW REJA.
Façade of the Audiencia.
Granada. XVII Century.

work. Figure 121 is a late reja from the façade of the Audiencia in Granada, finished in 1587 in the style of Herrera.

PULPITS

Wrought iron pulpits, several of which were mentioned in the Gothic period, became a favorite subject for the Renaissance ironworker, and played as

FIG. 124. SWINGING PULPIT.
Monastery of Las Huelgas, Burgos.
XVI Century.

FIG. 123. RENAISSANCE PULPIT.
Sevilla Cathedral.
Early XVI Century.

EASTON PUBLIC LIBRARY
EASTON PA

SMALLER RENAISSANCE PRODUCTIONS 107

great a part in the development of Spanish Renaissance as beautifully carved marble pulpits did in the Italian. The towns of Avila, Sevilla, Toledo, Burgos, Tortosa, Santiago contain the best known examples, usually in pairs. In mentioning the flamboyant pulpit of the capilla mayor in Avila Cathedral (Figure 40), its Renaissance companion was referred to (Frontispiece and Figure 122). This is hexagonal in plan and reached by a staircase which winds about the pier (for both pulpits set some distance forward of the reja). Not a detail of it but is of purest Renaissance. As sculpture it is equal to the celebrated pulpit by Benedetto de Majano, in Santa Croce, in Florence, but instead of being worked as a positive (from the face) as the marble was, the metal one had to be worked as a negative (hammered from the back), requiring greater skill on the part of the artizan. Unlike much of the repoussé already discussed, these panels are beaten from comparatively small sheets and riveted to the wooden frame upon which the whole is built. No attempt is made to conceal the joining of the sheets; on the contrary the rivet heads are accentuated into little features. The standard and the beautifully wrought supporting brackets are beaten in solid iron; an idea of the richness of the brackets and the underside of the pulpit can be best obtained by consulting the drawing used as a frontispiece. The stair, including the rail and stringer, was made considerably later by an inferior workman, and is somewhat out of scale with the body of the pulpit. If only Spain, when following Italy's art and architecture, had followed the excellent Italian custom of recording the creators of each fine production, it would be an added delight to those who now find the Spanish work so interesting. Little or nothing is known of the Avila rejero in question. Juan Francés is hazarded by some writers as the author of these pulpits as well as the capilla mayor reja. Whoever wrought them was a thorough artist, for portraits, figures, and ornament in every form were all handled with equal facility.

Of entirely different character, because much less sophisticated, are the two iron pulpits of the capilla mayor of Sevilla Cathedral. Figure 123 shows one, while its companion may be seen by referring to Figure 101, which illustration further shows how the two pulpits are actually part of the reja composition. By thus combining them, the skilful Friar Francisco de Salamanca offered the best solution for reaching the pulpit without disturbing its graceful chalice-like outline by the angularity of a visible staircase. Here the staircase is partly concealed behind the reja, and the priest, after ascending, passes through by means of the imperceptibly hinged five bars mentioned in the description of the capilla mayor reja. The Sevilla pulpits, while as beautiful as the Avila example, are less architectonic in design and exhibit more of a sculpturesque quality; the subjects of the panels are all drawn from biblical history. Particularly fine is the portion directly under the pulpit, and also the cylindrical standard covered with beautiful filigree ornamented. The Sevilla pulpits, like the rejas, are

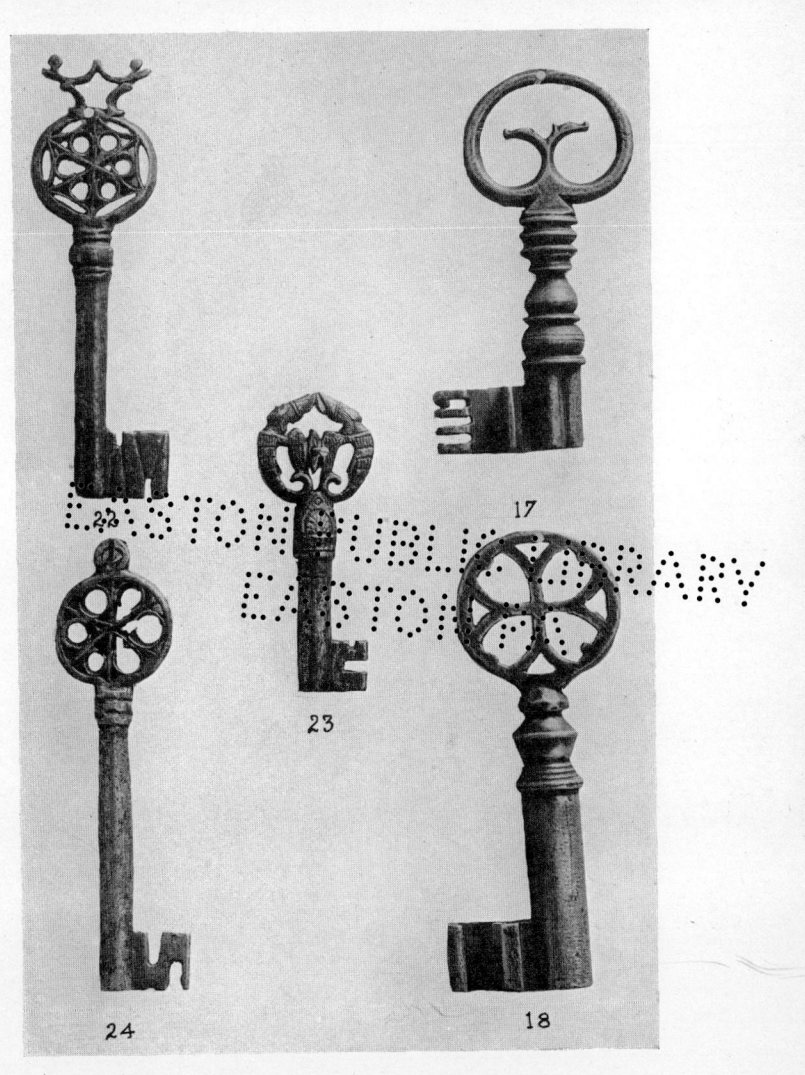

FIG. 127. SPANISH KEYS OF THE XVI, XVII,
AND XVIII CENTURIES.
Hispanic Society of America.
Nos. 17, 18, 22, 23, and 24.

EASTON PUBLIC LIBRARY
EASTON PA

FIG. 128. VARGUEÑO WITH DECORATIONS IN IRON.
XVI Century.
Hispanic Society of America.

EASTON PUBLIC LIBRARY
EASTON PA

heavily gilt and present an imposing appearance in the sombre cathedral. In the same class as to design are the fine ones by Villalpando made for Toledo in 1548; but these are worked in bronze, as indeed are many parts of the capilla mayor reja by the same artist.

Swinging pulpits are also found in Spain and one is illustrated from the monastery of Las Huelgas in Burgos (Figure 124). Though slightly out of the perpendicular, it is still in use. It is octagonal in form, with each face divided into four panels of equal size containing saints in relief. Practically no additional detail adorns it. The execution is good, but it is the novelty of not being supported on a pedestal or standard, but swung from the wall on an iron bracket, that chiefly commands attention. To give access to the pulpit it was swung back to the wall and reached by a little portable staircase.

IRONWORK FOR DOORS AND CHESTS

It was not habitual in Spain, as in France, for the ironworker to lavish unlimited time and consummate skill on locks and keys. These objects therefor are not remarkable, though some are sufficiently rich. Among the best keys are the early ones made by the Moors; for with them the key was a great symbol to be placed as the emblem of vigilance or ownership on their gates and towers. Two of the most famous Moorish keys are those in Sevilla Cathedral (Figure 125) the larger being silver and the smaller iron. This latter measures six inches and the wards form an inscription in Arabic cufic characters of which several different translations have been made, among them the following: "To God belongs all empire and power." These keys are supposed to be the ones delivered by the Moors to King Fernando el Santo when he con-

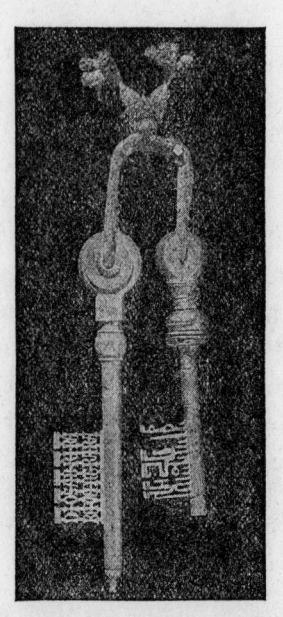

FIG. 125. MOORISH KEYS.
Sevilla Cathedral. Probably XII Century.

quered the city. This ceremony of giving up the keys of some long guarded and defended place probably occured in Spain more frequently than in any other country; hence in Spanish paintings, in stone and iron reliefs, and in carved wood, it was a favorite theme. Another interesting iron key with wards composed of lettering is in the possession of the Hispanic Society

FIG. 131. FACE OF VARGUEÑO SHOWING IRON MOUNTINGS.
XVI Century.
Hispanic Society of America.

EASTON PUBLIC LIBRARY
EASTON PA

SMALLER RENAISSANCE PRODUCTIONS 111

(Figure 126). This time the characters are Gothic and the inscription Spanish. The key is supposed to date from the fourteenth century and was found in Caspe in the province of Aragón.

In Renaissance days it was not the bit, but the

FIG. 126. GOTHIC KEY.
Aragonese. XIV Century.
Hispanic Society of America.
Length 8½ in.   No. 41.

bow of the key on which most care was expended, since this latter lent itself better to the curving and intertwined motifs of the period. Spanish Renaissance keys were better than the Italian but far inferior to the French, which were marvels of art. The most ornate Spanish examples were those given to the king's favorite ministers and admitting them to the royal apartments. "Under Charles II all the gentlemen of the king's household carried at all times gilt master-keys to every room of every royal palace, with absurdly large, oblong bow handles projecting from the right hand pocket and secured by colored ribbons. The valets carried the same key but it was not guilt. If a key was lost, the loser had to warn the chamberlain, who immediately caused every lock to be changed at a cost often exceeding 10,000 crowns which had to be defrayed by the loser. Dummy keys were given as badges to officials who had no occasion to use them, and to some noblemen not of the household as a mark of distinction. They are known to collectors as chamberlain's keys. There is a fine series of them in the British Museum, but they possess no artistic merit." (J. Starkie Gardner).

Figure 127 shows several keys in the Hispanic Society's collection, not ceremonial, but for everyday use. The one in the center of the page is closely patterned after the Dauphin keys of France, while the bows of the remainder (expecting No. 17) are cut in the flimsy Italian manner; that is, instead of the ornament being cut from the solid, it is made in small detached pieces which are inserted in the ring and held in place by means of solder and pins. It seems strange that the Spanish ironworker, who evinced supreme ability in meeting the many problems of the monumental reja, should have slighted a simple little commonplace like the key. In default of any illuminating records preserved from the period, the explanation is offered that it was the ambition of the most expert men to secure employment on rejas, which left the comparatively insignificant key to apprentices.

Locks, however, received considerably more attention and some distinctive ones were developed, especially on the Renaissance rejas and also on that peculiarly Spanish piece of furniture called the vargueño. The reja lockbox, or lock proper, was usually not so ornamented as its hasp and bolt, which, besides being decorated in divers ways, was monumental in size, with a hasp often as long as two feet and operating a formidable looking bar. Excellent examples of this type may be seen on the reja of the coro in Sevilla Cathedral and on that of the Royal Chapel at Granada.

In order to understand the importance of the vargueño lock (mentioned as especially worthy of attention) it requires some slight description of this national piece of furniture. It has been explained how in the Gothic periods the Spaniards had developed the chest into a distinctive article which they called the vargueño. The earliest Moorish examples found are richly inlaid with ivory, pearl, and various colored woods in the Eastern manner, leaving room for comparatively little decorative iron; but the same article, as developed and enlarged by the Spaniards, has a wooden exterior (generally walnut) of the simplest nature and depending solely on applied iron for its decorative effect. This piece of furniture was so plentifully and so well made in the little town of Vargas near Toledo that it received the name of vargueño. There is no doubt that its making must have given employment to many Moorish artizans still in Spain who carried out their own schemes of decoration, which accounts for the continued Oriental character of much of the applied metal work.

In shape the vargueño was an oblong box whose

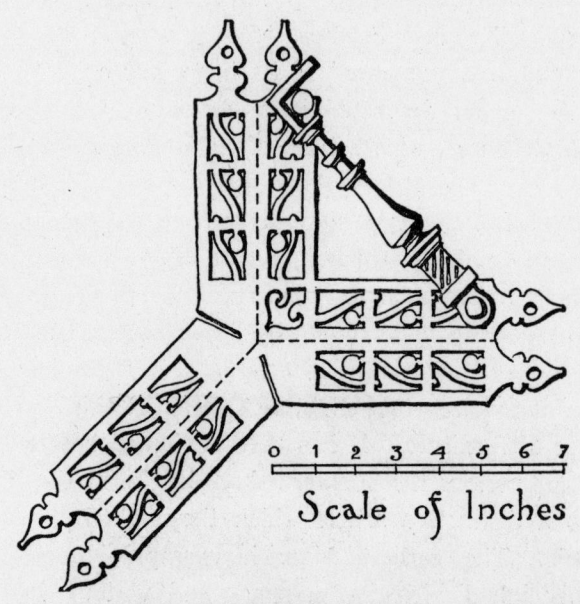

FIG. 129. FLATTENED OUT CORNER–BRACE OF A VARGUEÑO.

front let down on hinges, disclosing the drawers inside. It was mounted generally on a stand from which two massive supports pulled out to hold the front when let down, thus forming a sort of secretary (Figure 128). It became one of the most popular and distinctive bits of Spanish furniture, and was the *rai-*

FIG. 133. RUBBING FROM A VARGUEÑO LOCKPLATE.
XVII Century.
Hispanic Society of America. No. 127.
Height 9 in.

FIG. 132. RUBBING FROM A VARGUEÑO LOCKPLATE.
XVI Century.
Hispanic Society of America. No. 129.
Height 9 in.

EASTON PUBLIC LIBRARY
EASTON PA

SMALLER RENAISSANCE PRODUCTIONS 115

son d'être of various beautiful locks, lozenge shaped plaques, and interesting angle braces; which last, considering the excellent dovetailing of the woodwork at the ends would almost seem superfluous and were retained doubtless merely as an additional point of richness, especially in late Renaissance examples. Figure 129 is a drawing, developed in plan, a corner piece cut from a single sheet, along with its accompanying hook and eye. This latter feature and also the little push buttons at the sides of the front are designed to relieve the strain on the central hasp. But of all metal trimmings on the vargueño it was the lock and its hasp that received the most attention. Many were worked up to an extraordinary degree unlike any similar objects made in Europe. Figure 130 is a simple lock, twelve inches high, typical of the late sixteenth century; its fixing staples, in pairs and very much featured, are, along with the two flanking colonnettes of the hasp, the chief objects in relief. The colonnettes are furnished with a staple on the back so that a turn of the key throws a bolt through both. The filagree of the plate is backed with velours to obtain additional richness, and the iron is gilded to further accentuate the patterning. Other details on the face of vargueños were the two ornamental placques with pulls fastened to them and used when letting down the front (Figure 131). To obtain symmetry certain plaques were added that have no other purpose whatever; these generally used a bosse or a pilgrim's shell as a central motif. All practical features were firmly held to the wooden box by at least one huge nail driven through and turned over on the inside, and very little effort was made to conceal this crude method of fastening. The lock box was always mortised in the wood, the plate flush on the outside and nothing visible on the inside but

FIG. 130. VARGUEÑO LOCK.
XVI Century.
Hispanic Society of America.
Height 12 in.

the rivet heads. Three little iron shell heads on the outside generally indicated the location of the two hinges of the movable front. The sides of the vargueño were plainer than the front, the handles, often of beautiful design, being the only note aside from small corner bracings. Figures 132 to 135 are de-

FIG. 135. VARGUEÑO LOCKPLATE
WITH HASP.
XVII Century.
Hispanic Society of America.
Plate 9 in. square.   No. 134.

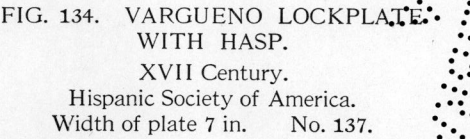

FIG. 134. VARGUEÑO LOCKPLATE
WITH HASP.
XVII Century.
Hispanic Society of America.
Width of plate 7 in.   No. 137.

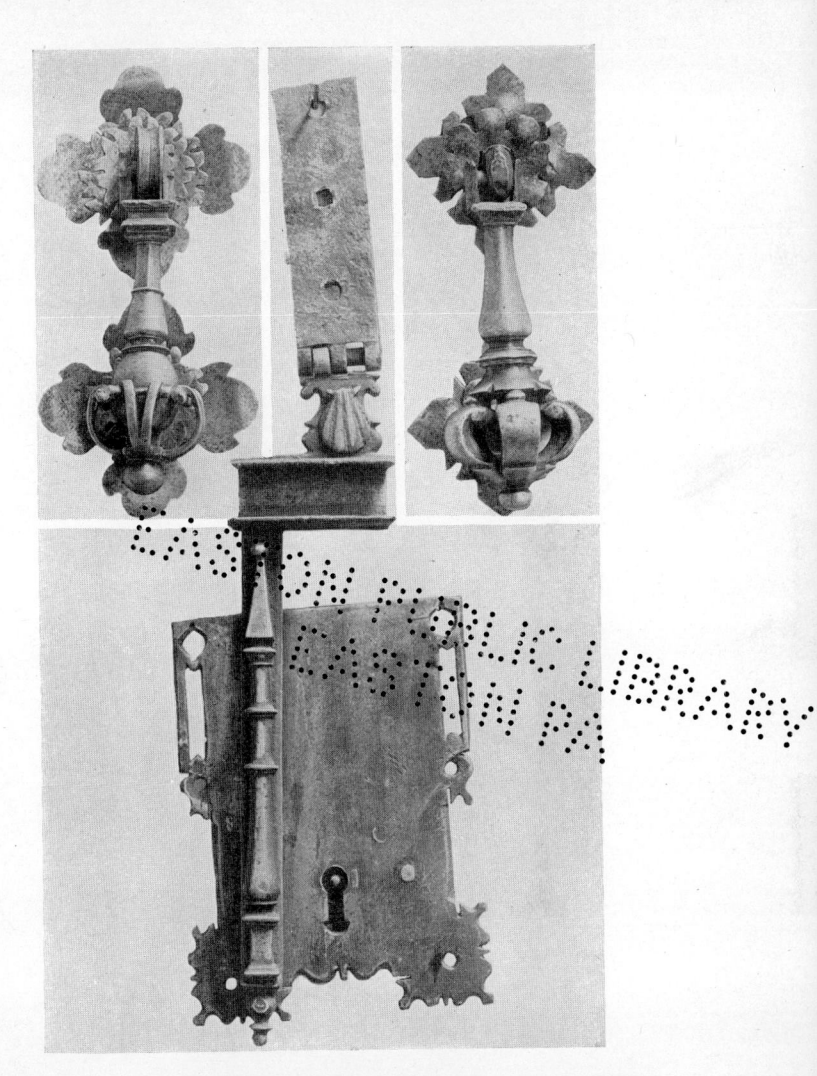

FIG. 137. A PAIR OF RENAISSANCE DOOR KNOCKERS.
XVII Century.   Hispanic Society of America.
Height 6 in.   Nos. 131 and 133.
FIG. 138. LOCKPLATE AND HASP.
XVII Century.   Hispanic Society of America.
Plate 5½ in. high.   No. 126.

EASTON PUBLIC LIBRARY
EASTON PA

tached vargueño locks in the Hispanic Society's collection, two still retaining their long, slender hasps. Of these examples Figure 132, a rubbing of a design derived, apparently, from the escutcheon of the owner, is a very superior piece of work; Figures 134 and 135 are typical Renaissance, yet the latter shows little study of conventional patterning, the design appearing as if it had been eaten out hap-hazard by an acid.

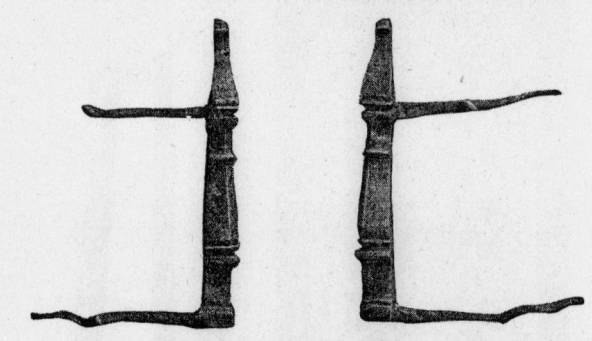

FIG. 136. A PAIR OF RENAISSANCE FIXING-STAPLES.
Hispanic Society of America.
Height 4 in.   No. 135.

Figure 136 is a pair of fixing staples showing how the form developed from the Gothic buttress.

Knockers became less of a feature in Spain in the sixteenth and seventeenth centuries, but never fell into such disuse as in other countries of Europe; in fact, the knocker is to this day a very much used piece of door hardware. As it became more utilitarian it was reduced in size but maintained its good workmanship. Figure 137 illustrates this type, the knocker in the shape of a little Renaissance baluster which is held forward from the door by a series of

118 SMALLER RENAISSANCE PRODUCTIONS

concentric rosette patterns interesting in relief. Figures 139 and 140 are very rare examples in that they exhibit the effect of the antique revival in Spain. This movement, generally ascribed to the excavations made at Pompeii, had a striking and lasting effect on European art. France, always most sensitive to art movements, welcomed it after her Louis XV extrava-

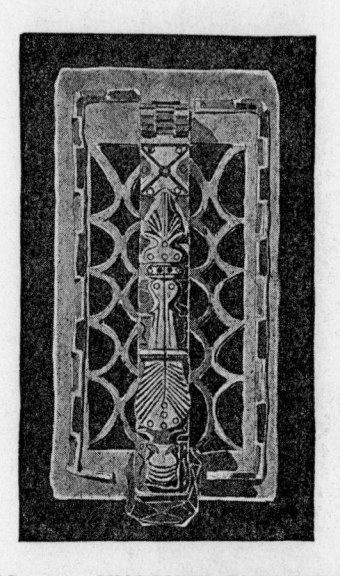

FIG. 139. KNOCKER EXHIBITING GREEK REVIVAL.
XVIII Century.
Hispanic Society of America.
Height 7 in.   No. 130.

gances and from there it passed with but little change into the neighboring countries. In the two knockers illustrating this phase in Spain, only the actual hammers show the feeling for the antique, the Greek acroteria being the principal motif for each. In other

FIG. 140. DOOR KNOCKER.
Renaissance backplate, hammer of Classic Inspiration.
Hispanic Society of America.
Height 13 in. No. 124.

portions of the hammer is seen a combination of Grecian and Spanish forms engraved into patterning, but the object, in spite of the change in ornamentation, retains its old form. In Figure 140 the backplate is purely Spanish with the supporting lions of León as its central motif and may be much earlier than the hammer, which dates from the middle of the eighteenth century. Of the same century are the door escutcheon and door pull from a palace in Palma de

FIG. 141. DOOR HANDLE AND ESCUTCHEON PLATE FROM A PALACE IN PALMA.
Balearic Isles. XVII Century.

Mallorca (Figure 141). These, in spite of the fact that Baroque obtained in the Balearic Islands, are very Spanish in character, cut from flat plates and with no surface finish whatever.

VII
THE LAST OF SPANISH IRONWORK

THE iron balcony, descendant of the purely defensive stone balcony, came into universal use in Spain in the late seventeenth century. It never, however, attained the excellence of the French examples of the same period designed by Lepautre and Marot, for by this time things had ceased to be done in Spain on a lavish scale. There are numerous isolated examples of the French style, but the smith instead of appreciating its elegance and comparative restraint, exaggerated its worst features. Occasionally, however, superior pieces are found and while largely French in character there is sufficient deviation in them to indicate that their maker was not executing his work in a merely perfunctory manner. Figures 142 and 143 are wrought iron balconies from Palma de Mallorca. (This handsome little island capital contains a surprising amount of interesting Renaissance architecture and is worth a visit for much more than its ironwork, in which particular field it was celebrated from earliest times, the Morey family of the fourteenth and fifteenth century having executed a quantity of fine early Gothic work.) In the majority of early Spanish balconies the spindle form was preferred (Figures 144 and 145); and the result, while severe in comparison with the rich Ba-

FIGS. 144 and 145. BALCONIES WITH SCROLL BRACKETS. Salamanca. XVIII Century.

EASTON PUBLIC LIBRARY
EASTON PA

THE LAST OF SPANISH IRONWORK

roque forms in French balconies, was never poor; perhaps because the spindles, always beaten out by hand, had as a consequent, variety which considerably enlivened them. Moreover, balconies were invariably upheld by long graceful scrolls, survivors of genuine forging, which were rarely if ever beaten

FIG. 142. BALCONY FRONT FROM A PALACE IN PALMA.
XVIII Century.

FIG. 143. BALCONY WITH A CURVED FRONT.
Palace in Palma. XVIII Century.

from the square as in other countries, but were round and spindled at the middle. A succession of these scroll-supported balconies makes the façade of even the plainest house attractive. Sometimes a single balcony extends clear across the house, as later in France; this is the case on the Hospital Real, erected about 1500, in Santiago, where the corbels are not of iron but of carved stone. In the little town of Santa Coloma de Queralt, in northern Catalonia, is another long balcony with not only iron supports but also interesting overhead braces embellished with dragon heads (Figure 146). It is dated 1760 and is a

FIG. 146. BALCONY WITH OVERHEAD BRACES.
Santa Coloma de Queralt, Catalonia. Dated 1760.

remarkably good piece of work for this late period. In the Casa Consistorial of Palma, built a century earlier, may be seen a long balcony where the railing is merely a spindle silhouette cut from sheet metal. This motif is rarely seen on the mainland, but in Palma it is used freely both for balconies and stair-rails (Figure

FIG. 148. ARMADURA OR WELL CRANE. Palma. XVII Century.

FIG. 147. IRON STAIR–BALUSTRADE. Patio of the Palacio Oleza. Palma.

EASTON PUBLIC LIBRARY
EASTON PA

147). The decorative value of this simple and inexpensive motif is surprising.

In this same illustration may be noticed an iron well-pulley (*armadura*) numbers of which may still be seen in the patios of the land. Figure 148 is also from Palma. While most of the *armaduras* date from

FIG. 149. TYPICAL IRON BRACKET.
Hispanic Society of America.
Height 3 ft. 4 in.   No. 175.

the beginning of the Renaissance, a few fine Gothic ones may be found through Catalonia in ancient palaces and castles. In quite the other side of the peninsula, Plasencia, is a curious standard in the Archbishop's garden. The well-curb here is T-shaped, made up of three sarcophogus-like troughs, and over

124 THE LAST OF SPANISH IRONWORK

each extends a dragon arm with pulley radiating from the tall iron standard; the whole structure is probably seventeenth century. Another unusual one, part Gothic and part Renaissance, is in the palace of the Count of Grajal, near León.

A large number of miscellaneous objects in iron

FIG. 150. CRUZ DE LINDE OR BOUNDARY CROSS.
Catalan. XV Century.

may be encountered by the traveler in Spain, from small decorative cooking utensils, such as the gridiron (Figure 153) to large iron frames on palaces and public buildings, in which their bells were hung. A particularly well-known bell apparatus is the ornate fourteenth-century one on the northeast tower of Barcelona Cathedral. Such superstructures form picturesque silhouettes against the sky as may be observed on hundreds of small churches throughout the land and

THE LAST OF SPANISH IRONWORK 125

even in Southern France. Fantastic iron weather vanes and finials are also seen; monumental among the former (but in bronze) is the figure on the former Moorish prayer tower, now the belfry of Sevilla Cathedral, representing Faith holding the banner of Constantine; it was cast in 1568 by Bartolomé Morel. This is the famous "Giraldillo" which gives the tower its name, and which moves quite readily with the wind in spite of the fact that it is thirteen feet high and weighs one and one-quarter tons. Iron crosses are frequently found, both on and in churches; those on the wayside, often in the nature of a boundary mark, are more rare (Figure 150).

In the making of Spanish tables, chairs and benches (which were not plentiful until French fashions were imported with the Bourbons), iron was often a structural adjunct, such as diagonal bracing and connecting pieces, corner angles, and nailheads. Not that the Spanish cabinet-maker was not thoroughly conscientious in his work, for Spanish furniture is as solidly constructed as any other of the period; but he was so imbued with the importance of iron that without its introduction he could not see his work satisfactorily finished. Figure 151 shows a common Spanish method of bracing a table with iron. In the case of benches the iron brace was in the form of a long hook which, when released from its eye, permitted the legs of the bench to fold, thereby increasing its portability. The bench is a really important article in Spanish interiors, and often exhibits, besides the brace, delicate little plaques of ornamental iron let into the back. Some-

126 THE LAST OF SPANISH IRONWORK

times it is covered with leather fastened down with ornamental nailheads, these in the form of shells, stars, crosses and rosettes.

Furniture entirely of iron exists, although such pieces, with the exception of iron beds, were unusual. In the well known collection of Señor Santiago Rusiñol at Sitjes, Catalonia, there is a rare and curious iron desk with leather fittings. Figure 152 shows a seventeenth-century iron chair, one of a set of twelve, four

FIG. 151. TABLE WITH WROUGHT IRON BRACES.
Hispanic Society of America.

of which are in the possession of the Hispanic Society. The entire chair is practically a wooden conception carried out in iron. It is well hammered up but presents nothing new in design excepting the back, which is conceived in the spirit of ironwork and makes a graceful contrast to the heavier structural members. Another iron chair, but designed in the spirit of the material, is the well known example among the Spanish pieces in the South Kensington Museum made entirely of pierced and inlaid (damascened) iron. It is a late but splendid specimen of the art, dating from

FIG. 154. SPANISH BIT WITH ORNAMENTS TO
WARD OFF THE EVIL EYE.
XVII Century.   Hispanic Society of America.   No. 132.
FIG. 155. SPUR OF A CONQUISTADOR.
XVI Century.   Hispanic Society of America.
Dia. of wheel 5½ in.   No. 139.
FIG. 156. STIRRUP OF A CONQUISTADOR.
XVI Century.   Hispanic Society of America.
Total length 18 in.   No. 140.

EASTON PUBLIC LIBRARY
EASTON PA

THE LAST OF SPANISH IRONWORK 127

the seventeenth or early eighteenth century. The art of damascening — incising the metal in a pattern into which is pressed gold or silver thread — was introduced into Spain by the Moors with whom the practice, presumably originating in Damascus, was very ancient. As early as the twelfth and thirteenth

FIG. 152. ONE OF FOUR IRON CHAIRS OF THE XVII CENTURY.
Hispanic Society of America.
Nos. 171, 172, 173 and 174.

centuries Moorish towns, — Almeria, Murcia, Sevilla, Granada, — were celebrated for it, and to this day the art is practiced in Spain. An Arab traveler, Al Makari, wrote of Murcia "the objects made there of iron, consisting of knives and scissors inlaid in gold,

128 THE LAST OF SPANISH IRONWORK

and other utensils fit either for the outfit of a bride or a soldier are in such large quantities that the mere thought of them confuses the imagination." Perhaps the best known modern work in damascening is the monument to Gen. Prim in Madrid. Other comparatively recent examples are the extra-

FIG. 153. CATALAN GRIDIRON.
XVII Century.

ordinary inlays in the royal palaces of Aranjuez and El Escorial.

The last phase of Spanish architecture, and a lamentable one, is the *Churrigueresco* of the late seventeenth century, named after the architect Churriguera who indulged in a delirium of ornament to conceal

FIG. 157. GRILLE IN MARKET. Granada. Late XVIII Century.

FIG. 158. DOOR IRONWORK OF THE CASA CONSISTORIAL. Barcelona. Late XIX Century.

the faultiness of his structures. These grandiose productions were the Spanish interpretation of the French Baroque, and the iron accessories used were close but inferior to their French prototypes, as may be seen in the balconies of the fantastic façade of the palace of the Marqués de Dos Aguas in Valencia. The few rejas now erected took on an entirely new character; instead of spindles and embossed bands as motifs, they were adorned with cartouches, medallions, and a quantity of capricious scrolling. This was the period that gave to France and England those eighteenth century gateways which stand as monuments to the virility of late ironworkers; but in Spain, owing to the concentration of domestic life within the patio, and also to the lack of villa life, there never was the demand for exterior gates. In Sevilla and certain other Andalusian towns, however, the arrangement of the houses necessitated iron gates, called *canceles*, to the patio. As the street doors are thrown open day and evening, the passerby catches many a glimpse of these Baroque gates and the attractive patio beyond. An isolated display of late exterior ironwork may be seen at La Granja, the royal park created in imitation of Versailles by Spain's first Bourbon king, Philip V. These accessories, like the gardens they adorn, are in no sense a Spanish expression. It was probably all designed and executed by French artists, and exhibits Baroque in more pleasing aspect than is found elsewhere in Spain, except, as already stated, in Palma de Mallorca. Figure 157 shows a typical bit of late eighteenth-century Spanish ironwork in Granada.

130 THE LAST OF SPANISH IRONWORK

There is nothing particularly Spanish about it; it could have been produced in any other European country at the time.

Until very recent years modern Spanish ironwork gave no signs of improvement. All that was bad in the ornamentation of the French Napoleon III style was copied by Spanish artizans of the late nineteenth century. Figure 158, part of the iron fittings on the modern doors of the restored façade of the Casa Consistorial at Barcelona, shows the hard spiky forms so characteristic of this period; but the same city has since produced some excellent works, an encouraging sign that in Catalonia at least there may be some return to those splendid traditions which gave sixteenth-century Spanish ironwork a high place among the fine arts.

INDEX

A

Acuña, Bishop de, 36
Aldabón, 46
Alcalá, de Henares, 104
Al Makari, 127
Almería, 127
Alhambra, 15
Amarejo, 2
Andalucía, 12, 129
Andino, Pedro de, 85
Andino, Cristóbal de, 85, 91, 94, 96
Anaya grille, Salamanca, 33, 35
Andirons, 67
Antique revival, 99, 118
Aragonese, 56, 64
Aranjuez, 128
Arcón, 60
Arenas, Hernando de, 97
Arquetas, 61
Armor, 100
Armorial bearings, 37, 39, 73
Armadura, 123
Avila, 27, 51, 96, 107

B

Backplate, 46, 49, 52, 54
Baggage chests, 60
Balcony, 99, 120
Balustrade, 99
Barcelona, 20, 52
—— Cathedral, 20, 21, 72, 124
Barcelona, Casa Consistorial, 130
—— Santa Maria del Mar, 19
Baroque, 98, 129
Bartolomé, Maestre, 85, 89
Basilicas, Christian, 9, 97
Basque, 49
Bell frames, 124
Bermudez, Ceán, 86
Blast furnace, 2, 4
Blazon, 37, 39, 90, 91
Bloom, 4
Boina, 49
Bosse, 16, 46, 49
Box fittings, 60
Bravo, Francisco, 83
Braziers, 62
Burgos, 20
—— Cathedral, 20, 36, 91
——, Las Huelgas, 109
——, Miraflores, 36, 86
Byzantine, 17

C

Cadiz, 97
Candelabra, 35, 62, 91
Candelero, 62
Candlestick, 62
Capilla del Condestable, Burgos, 77, 92
—— del Sagrario, Palencia, 11
—— de la Antigua, Sevilla, 85
—— de la Anunciación, Sevilla, 85

Capilla de la Concepción, Sevilla, 85
—— de la Gamba, Sevilla, 85
—— de la Presentación, Burgos, 91
—— de los Caballeros, Cuenca, 97
—— de los Reyes Nuevos, Toledo, 82
—— de los Reyes Viejos, Toledo, 82
—— de N. S. de Blanca, Palencia, 96
—— de N. S. de la Piedad, Segovia, 97
—— de N. S. de las Angustias, Palencia, 25
—— de San Pedro, Palencia, 93, 95
—— de Santa Ana, Burgos, 36
—— de Santa Cruz, Pamplona, 10
—— de Santa Librada, Sigüenza, 80
—— de Santa Magdalena, Tarragona, 82
—— Mozárabe, Toledo, 82
—— Mayor, Alcalá, 98
—— Mayor, Cuenca, 97
—— Mayor, Osma, 96
—— Mayor, Palencia, 93
—— Mayor, Pamplona, 24
—— Mayor, Sevilla, 85
—— Mayor, Toledo, 73, 83
—— Real, Granada, 32, 72, 89
—— Real, Sevilla, 84
Cantabrian Provinces, 9
Canceles, 129
Caskets, 60
Cast iron, 5
Castile, 12
Catalonia, 2, 14, 67, 130
Catalan forge, 2, 4

Celtiberian sword, 1
Céspedes, Domingo de, 82
Celma, Juan Bautista, 99
Chairs in iron, 126
Charles II, 112
Charles V, 89, 90, 100
Chatón, 15
Chest fittings, 60, 113
Churriguera, 128
Churrigueresco, 128
Cluniacs, 8, 9
Colonnettes, 69
Coloring of iron, 38
Córdova, Mosque of, 17
Coro, its development, 76
——, Palencia Cathedral, 95
——, Plasencia Cathedral, 99
——, Sevilla Cathedral, 85, 87
——, Toledo Cathedral, 83
Covarrubias, Alonzo de, 83
Cresting, 40, 86, 90
Crusades, 13
Cruz de linde, 125
Cutlery, 127
Cuenca, 85, 96

D

Damascening, 126
Damascus, 127
Delgado, Juan, 85
Diagonal lattice, 27
Door ironwork, 14, 45, 52
Doors plated with iron, 18, 45
Domestic utensils, 2, 62
Dos Aguas, Marqués de, 129

E

Eastern influence, 52
Ebro, 3, 12, 47
Egas, Enrique de, 69, 89
Embossed work, 90
Escalera Dorada, 93

INDEX

Escorial, 128
Escutcheon plate, 14
Estremadura, 44

F

Ferdinand, 89, 90, 94
Fernando el Santo, 20, 76, 91, 110
Fire dogs, 67
—— guards, 67
—— screens, 67, 68
Fixing staples, 57, 115
Flamboyant, 36, 41, 54
Flemish influence, 43, 63, 94
Florence, 75, 107
Fonseca, Alonzo de, 94, 98
Font cranes, 123
Francés, Juan, 43, 71, 82, 98, 108
Francisco de Salamanca, 85, 86, 108
French Gothic, 45
—— hinges, 46
—— balconies, 121
—— keys, 111, 112
—— locks, 56, 109
Furnace, open hearth, 3
—— Catalan forge, 2, 4

G

Gardner, J. Starkie, 7, 70, 71, 112
Gates, 102
German influence, 35, 36, 37, 59
Gerona Cathedral, 20
Gestoso y Perez, 76
Gilding of iron, 38
Giralda tower, 87, 125
Gotico-florido ironwork, 32, 40, 54, 94
Gothic style, 20
Granada, 25, 32, 76, 104, 127
—— Audiencia, 106

Granada Cathedral, 89
——, Capilla Real, 32, 72, 77, 89
Granja, La, 129
Gridiron, 128
Grilles, 9
—— English, 9
—— French, 9, 11
—— Roman, 9
—— Oriental, 12
Greek revival, 99, 118
Grajal, Count of, 124
Guadalupe, 87, 96

H

Hachero, 64
Handrail of iron, 122
Hasps, 56, 59
Helve hammer, 7
Heraldry, 37, 39, 77, 90
Hinges, 45
Hood of knocker, 46
Horizontal member, 39, 74
Hospital de Santa Cruz, Toledo, 69, 102
—— Real, Santiago, 69, 121
Huche, 61
Huesca, 19
Human figure in iron, 29, 70, 74, 89
Herrera, 106

I

Idrobo, Diego de, 85
Interlaced grilles, 27
Isabella, 89, 90, 94
Italian influence, 69, 75, 77

J

Jaén, 90

K

Keys, 109
—— chamberlain, 112

INDEX

Keys, French, 111, 112
—— Gothic, 111
—— Italian, 111, 112
—— master, 112
—— Moorish, 109
—— Renaissance, 111
—— Spanish, 111
Knockers, 14, 15, 117

L

León, 11, 124
León Cathedral, 20, 81
——, N. S. del Mercado, 11
Lepoutre, 120
Le Puy-en-Velay, 9
Llamador, 46
Locks, 56, 109
—— French, 56, 109
—— Gothic, 56
—— Renaissance, 116
—— Spanish, 56

M

Madrid, 17
——, Museo, Nacional, 17, 61
——, Armería, 101
——, statue of General Prim, 128
Malaga, 96
Malleable iron, 3, 5
Manresa Cathedral, 20
Margaret of Spain, 61
Marot, 120
Marseille, 1
Medina de Rioseco, 93
Mendoza, Cardinal, 102
Miraflores, Convent of, 36, 86
Morel, Bartolomé, 125
Morey family, 120
Moors, 2, 8
Moorish doors, 45
—— influence, 12, 52
Moorish bronze work, 17

Moorish ironwork, 18
Mudéjar style, 13, 53
—— doors, 17
Muñez Sancho, 85, 97
Murcia, 127

N

Nailhead, 14, 46
Nails, 15
Napoleon, 83
—— III, 130
Navarre, 10, 14

O

Oil immersion, 7
Open hearth, 3
Orfèvrerie, 73
Oriental influence, 12, 13, 52
Osma, 96, 98
Oviedo, 96

P

Painting of iron, 38
Palencia, Antonio de, 85
—— 11, 94
—— Cathedral, 11, 93
——, San Pablo, 25
Palma de Mallorca, 119, 120, 129
—— de Mallorca, Casa Consistorial, 122
Paular, Chartreuse of, 86
Pamplona, 10, 20, 24
—— Cathedral, 24
Pedro Davila's house, 27
Peñafiel, Louis de, 82
Philip V, 129
Pilasters, 72
Pilgrim shell, 50, 115
Plasencia, 123
—— Cathedral, 96, 99
Plateresque style, 69, 77
Pierced lettering, 34, 35

INDEX

Pompeii, 118
Prehistoric ironwork, 1
Prentice, Andrew, 97
Prieto, Fernando, 85
Pulpits, Gothic, 42
—— Avila Cathedral, 42
—— Burgos, San Gil, 42
—— Cortejana, San Salvador, 44
—— Murcia Cathedral, 44
—— Renaissance, 84, 106
—— Avila Cathedral, 107
—— Burgos, Monastery of Las Huelgas, 109
—— Sevilla Cathedral, 87, 108
—— Toledo Cathedral, 108
Pyrenean Provinces, 9, 51

R

Reja, 9
Rejero, 20
Relojero, Juan, 96
Renaissance style, 51, 69, 78
—— church rejas, 80
Repoussé, 40, 107
Rodriguez, Bartolomé, 82
—— Gaspar, 95, 96
Romanesque style, 8
—— rejas, 8
Romans, 1, 9, 62
Rusiñol Santiago, 126
Rust, prevention of, 7

S

Salamanca, 27
——, Catedral Vieja, 35
——, Casa de las Conchas, 27, 33
——, Archiepiscopal Palace, 27
—— University, 72, 102
Santa Colma de Queralt, 122
—— Croce, Florence, 197
—— Maria del Mar, Barcelona, 19

San Pablo, Palencia, 25
—— Clemente, Rome, 77
—— Millan, Segovia, 46
—— Vincente, Avila, 11
Santiago de Compostella, 34, 121
Saracenic influence, 11, 13
Segovia, 51, 96, 97
—— Cathedral, 103
——, Duque de, collection, 58, 97
Sevilla, 25, 87, 127
—— Cathedral, 39, 84, 108
——, Casa de Pilatos, 75, 104
——, Giralda tower, 87, 125
Sheathed doors, 18, 45
Sheathed columns, 72, 88, 90
Siloe, Diego de, 93
Silva, Francisco de, 82
Sigüenza, 30, 80
—— Cathedral, 37, 72
Smelting, 2
Smiths
—— Andino, Cristobal de, 85, 91, 94
—— Andino, Pedro de, 85
—— Arenas, Hernando de, 97
—— Bartolomé, Maestre, 85, 89
—— Bravo, Francisco, 83
—— Celma, Juan Bautista, 99
—— Céspedes, Domingo, 82
—— Delgado, Juan, 85
—— Francés, Juan, 42, 82, 98
—— Francisco de Salamanca, 85, 108
—— Idrobo, Diego de, 85
—— Morey, Juan, 120
—— Morey, Pedro, 120
—— Muñez Sancho, 85
—— Palencia, Antonio de, 85
—— Peñafiel, Louis de, 82
—— Prieto, Fernando, 85
—— Rodriguez, Bartolomé, 82
—— Rodriguez, Gaspar, 95, 96
—— Silva, Francisco de, 82

INDEX

—— Villalpando, Francesco de, 82
—— Urisarri, Lopez de, 96
—— Yepes, Juan de, 85
—— Relojero, Juan, 96
South Kensington Museum, 126
Spindles, 32, 69, 70
Split bar, 31
Simon of Cologne, 36
St. Sernin, Toulouse, 21
St. Swithin grille, Winchester, 9
Steel, 5
Street, George, 18, 24, 74
Strozzi Palace, Florence, 75
Superimposing of plates, 40, 41
Swords, 1

T

Table braces, 125
Tarragona Cathedral, 18, 82
Threaded work, 22, 40
Toledo, 25, 27, 82
—— Cathedral, 20, 27, 45
—— Count of, 34, 105
—— Hospital de Santa Cruz, 69, 102
Tomb rails, 35, 36
Tools, 78
Tortosa, 96
Toro, 26
Torch holders, 64
Toulouse, 21
Tuyère, 4

U

Urisarri, Lopez de, 96

V

Valencia, 96
Varga, 113
Vargueño, 113
Vasari, 75
Venice, 17
Venetian grilles, 17
Vergas, 14, 35
Vertical bars, 21, 29
Vich, 11
—— Museum, 11, 51, 62, 64
Villalpando, Francesco de, 87
Viollet-le-Duc, 21
Visigoths, 2, 8, 16

W

Weather vanes, 125
Welding, 5, 71
Well cranes, 123
Window rejas, 25, 103

Y

Yepes, Juan de, 85

Z

Zamora, 36
Zaragoza, 96, 100
Zapata, Don Gonzalo, 95

CATALOGUE OF IRONWORK IN THE COLLECTION OF THE HISPANIC SOCIETY OF AMERICA

NUMBER

1– 2 Decorative nails or bosses, Moorish half-orange type.

3– 9 Decorative door bosses with separate nails, XV and XVI Century.

10– Moorish bosse with fixed nail.

11– Spanish bosse with separate nail.

12– Moorish bosse with fixed nail.

13– 14 Moorish nails from a door in the Alhambra, Granada.

15– 18 Typical keys of the XVII Century.

19– 20 Ornamental door bosses, XVI Century.

21– 25 Keys, XVI and XVII Century.

26– 34 Various types of nails from the XV to the XVII Century.

35– 40 Spanish door bosses of Moorish design.

41– Aragonese key, XIV Century.

42– 46 Elaborate door bosses, Moorish or half-orange type.

47– Door knocker, earliest appearance of flat crown design, about 1400.

48– Door knocker, first appearance of half-crown motif.

CATALOGUE OF THE COLLECTION

49– 50   Door knockers, half crown motif, XVI Century.
51–   Door knocker, flat crown design, XVII Century.
52–   Door knocker, entirely forged, XV Century.
53– 54   Detached hammers of knockers, XVI Century.
55–   Door knocker with incised patterning, XV Century.
56–   Door knocker with incised patterning, XVI Century.
57– 58   Bosses used as backplates for knockers, Moorish design, XV Century.
59– 60   Bosses, Moorish patterning.
61– 64   Door ring handles with clinch, XV and XVI Century.
65–   Hammer of Knocker.
66–   Ring handle with bosse and clinch, XVI Century.
67–   Detached hammer of knocker, probably XV Century.
68–   Door ring handle, Moorish in character, XV Century.
69–   Door knocker, Moorish design, XV Century.
70–   Gothic door knocker, split bar type, XVI Century.
71– 73   Pair of door knockers, Gothic in spirit, XV Century.
72–   Door ring handle, Mudéjar (Gothic-Moorish), XVI Century.
74–   Gothic door knocker, stirrup pattern, XV Century.
75–   Door knocker with pilgrim shell, XVII Century.
76–   Pair of striker heads, XVII Century.

CATALOGUE OF THE COLLECTION 139

77– Door ring handle, Moorish in character, XV Century.
78– Bosse backplate of a knocker, XVII Century.
79– Door ring knocker, Mudéjar, XV Century.
80– 81 Pair of ring knockers, Gothic, XV Century.
82– Door ring knocker, Moorish in character, XV Century.
83– Door ring handle, Mudéjar, XVI Century.
84– Pilgrim shell knocker, XVI Century.
85– Door ring knocker, Mudéjar, XV Century.
86– Door knocker, Mudéjar, XVII Century.
87– Door knocker, stirrup pattern, Mudéjar, XVII Century.
88– Detached hammer of a knocker, XVI Century.
89– Door ring handle, Moorish in character, XVI Century.
90– Detached hammer of a knocker, XVII Century.
91– Door ring knocker, Moorish in character, XVI Century.
92– Detached hammer of a knocker, XVI Century.
93– Door ring knocker, XVII Century.
94– Detached hammer of a door knocker, XVII Century.
95– Door ring handle, example of rich Mudéjar, XVI Century.
96– Door knocker, star pattern in rich Mudéjar, XVI Century.
97 Door ring knocker, Moorish in character, XVI Century.
98– Detached striker of a knocker.

99– Door ring knocker, Moorish in character, XVII Century.
100– Door knocker, backplate, and fixing staples, XVII Century.
101– Door knocker, XVII Century.
102– Door knocker and handle, XVII Century.
103– Door knocker, stirrup pattern, Mudéjar, XVII Century.
104– Door knocker with Moorish bosse, XVI Century.
105– Late Gothic plaque worked in repoussé.
106– Door knocker, Gothic in spirit, XVI Century.
107– Gothic lockplate.
108– Lock and hasp with false fixing staple over keyhole. XVI Century.
109– Lock and hasp with false fixing staple over keyhole, XVI Century.
110– Door knocker, late Gothic in style, XVII Century.
111– Door knocker, French flamboyant in character, late XVI Century.
112– Gothic lock with curious hasp, XV Century.
113– Chest lock, XVI Century.
114– Lock-box and hasp in rich Mudéjar style, probably XVII Century.
115– Lockplate and hasp, Renaissance, XVII Century.
116– Small detached hammer of a door knocker.
117– Door knocker, Gothic in spirit but probably XVIII Century.
118– Lock with slide-plate, Gothic, XV Century.

CATALOGUE OF THE COLLECTION 141

119– Lockplate and hasp, XVI Century.
120– Detached hammer of a door knocker.
121– Chest lock and hasp, Renaissance, XVI Century.
122– Door knocker, Renaissance, early XVII Century.
123– Door knocker, Aragonese in type, XVII Century.
124– Knocker, backplate Renaissance, hammer Greek revival, XVIII Century.
125– Door knocker, Aragonese in type, XVII Century.
126– Lock and hasp, Renaissance, XVII Century.
127– Chest lock and hasp, XVII Century.
128– Door knocker, XVII Century.
129– Vargueño lockplate and hasp, Renaissance, XVI Century.
130– Door knocker, Greek revival, XVIII Century.
131–133 Pair of door knockers, Renaissance, XVII Century.
132– Spanish bit with ornaments for warding off the evil eye. XVII Century.
134– Vargueño lockplate and hasp, Renaissance, XVII Century.
135– Pair of Renaissance fixing staples, XVI Century.
136– Detached hammer of a knocker, XVIII Century.
137– Vargueño lockplate and hasp, Renaissance, XVII Century.
138– Door knocker, Renaissance, XVII Century.

CATALOGUE OF THE COLLECTION

139– Spur of a Conquistador, XVI Century.
140– Stirrup of a Conquistador, XVI Century.
141– Pocket-knife.
142– Door knocker, Renaissance, XVII Century.
143– Heraldic cartouche, beaten in repoussé and colored. XVII Century.
144– Repoussé band from a reja, Renaissance, XVI Century.
145– Pierced band from a reja, Gothic, XV Century.
146– Repoussé band from a reja, Renaissance, XVI Century.
147– Tracery band built up of two plates, Gothic, XV Century.
148– Repoussé band from a reja, Renaissance, XVI Century.
149– Tracery band built up of two plates, Gothic, XV Century.
150– Pierced band from a reja, Renaissance, XVI Century.
151– Repoussé band from a reja, Renaissance, XVI Century.
152– Repoussé band from a reja, Renaissance, XVI Century.
153– Pierced band from a reja, Gothic, XV Century.
154– Pair of foliated sprigs, Renaissance, XVII Century.
155– Pierced band from a reja, Renaissance, XVI Century.
156– Repoussé band with delicate figures, Renaissance, XVI Century.

CATALOGUE OF THE COLLECTION 143

157– Repoussé band from a reja, Renaissance, early XVI Century.
158– Repoussé band, dolphin pattern, Renaissance, XVI Century.
159– Pierced band from a reja, Gothic, XV Century.
160– Crude border in three pieces.
161– Celtiberian sword, found at Amarejo.
162–163 Pair of ecclesiastical candelabras, XVI Century.
164– Two storied brazier, XVII Century.
165–168 Four spindles and their pedestals, from a reja, XVI Century.
169– Incomplete cresting of a reja, from northern Spain, XVII Century.
170– Pair of gates, XVII Century.
171–174 Set of four iron chairs of the XVII Century.
175–176 Pair of brackets, XVII Century.
177– Iron strong box.
178–179 Pair of crowning pinnacles, XV Century.
180– Portion of a Gothic arch, XV Century.